Dear Frien...

I'd like to take this opportunity to personally thank you for visiting one of our 56 branches to pick up this edition of "American Savings Library of International Cooking." May it provide you, your family and friends many hours of pleasant dining.

We hope these books will always remind you that there is ALWAYS something "cooking" at American Savings. We can provide you with the highest quality ingredients available to anyone, including:

★ **SAFETY SINCE 1885**

★ **CAPITAL AND RESERVES <u>OVER</u> <u>TWICE</u> LEGAL REQUIREMENTS**

★ **ASSETS OVER 3 <u>BILLION</u> DOLLARS STRONG**

★ **NATION'S <u>HIGHEST</u> <u>INTEREST</u> ON INSURED SAVINGS**

★ **MANY FREE SERVICES WITH SPECIFIED MINIMUM BALANCES**

★ **56 CONVENIENT LOCATIONS**

★ **PLEASANT AND HELPFUL PERSONNEL TO SERVE YOU**

We know you will find these ingredients to your liking, and that is why American Savings is one of the NATION'S LARGEST financial institutions.

Remember, at American Savings YOU *NEVER* LOSE, YOU *ALWAYS* GAIN! And, Bon Appétit!

Sincerely,

S. Mark Taper

S. Mark Taper, President

AMERICAN SAVINGS AND LOAN ASSOCIATION
FOUNDED 1885

The recipes in this book have been grill-tested or spit-tested and then taste-tested by the staff of home economists of Tested Recipe Institute, who have made a specialty of the fine art of barbecuing and outdoor cooking. Under the supervision of Lillian C. Ziegfeld, the testing was done by Mabel Stolte and Frances Hoffman on all types of equipment and all through the year. The book was written with the idea that barbecuing is an art to enjoy the year 'round and not a pleasure to confine to the short warm weather season.

The Art of Barbecue and Outdoor Cooking

By Tested Recipe Institute

BANTAM BOOKS

TORONTO · NEW YORK · LONDON

A NATIONAL GENERAL COMPANY

THE ART OF BARBECUE AND OUTDOOR COOKING

A Bantam Book / published May 1958
2nd printing .... June 1958   4th printing .... July 1960
3rd printing .... May 1959   5th printing .... July 1960
Bantam Reference Library edition published April 1963
7th printing ..... December 1963
Bantam Cookbook Shelf edition published May 1967
9th printing .... April 1969   10th printing ...... April 1970
11th printing .... April 1971

12th printing

Library of Congress Catalog Card Number: 58-9231

Published simultaneously in the United States and Canada

---

*Bantam Books are published by Bantam Books, Inc., a National
General company. Its trade-mark, consisting of the words "Bantam
Books" and the portrayal of a bantam, is registered in the United
States Patent Office and in other countries. Marca Registrada.
Bantam Books, Inc., 666 Fifth Avenue, New York, N.Y. 10019.*

PRINTED IN THE UNITED STATES OF AMERICA

TABLE OF CONTENTS

Food cooked out-of-doors always tastes better regardless of the kind of equipment you use. It can be a modestly priced unit, a costly, elaborate chrome- or copper-finished unit, a handsome brick structure built on your patio, or it can be only a few stones, a hole dug in the ground or a stationary unit at the picnic grounds. The food can be hot dogs, sizzling hamburgs, juicy steak or a crisp brown suckling pig. The result is always the same—food tastes better.

This book has been written with all kinds of equipment in mind. You may not be able to prepare all the recipes on the equipment of your choice, but no matter what kind of a unit you use, you'll find plenty of recipes which you can cook to give you a world of fun and pleasure.

If you are new at barbecuing, you may want to start with a small inexpensive unit. Our guess is, that once you have experienced the fun of cooking out-of-doors, the first small unit will seem inadequate and you will want to graduate to a larger and more elaborate unit. Our advice is that when you buy a larger unit, you should hold on to the small one. It will be invaluable as an auxiliary unit when you entertain a crowd.

In this book you will find hundreds of recipes—meats, salads and extra dishes to make a meal complete—descriptions of the various types of units, advice on fire building and fire control and countless suggestions for making any barbecue party, large or small, a success. In addition, there is a section on barbecuing for a crowd which includes special recommendations for an Hawaiian luau, a clam bake, chicken bake and pit barbecuing.

CHOOSING A BARBECUE UNIT

Shopping for a barbecue unit can be fun. But, because of the tremendous variety of units available and features which different manufacturers have included, selection of a unit may be difficult unless you know what to shop for. So, before you shop, it would be wise to analyze your particular needs so that your money is well spent.

First, how much do you want to spend? Units are available to fit every purse. There are small units which cost as little as a dollar. Larger and more elaborate ones cost as much as $300.

Where do you plan to do most of the barbecuing? For stay-at-homes, the most satisfactory units have the cooking surface at work height. It is convenient to have one equipped with wheels so you can move it easily to take advantage of the wind for fire control and wheel it to the garage for storage when barbecuing is done.

How many people will you usually cook for? If you entertain a crowd frequently, then consider one of the larger units. Or, you may find it to your advantage to have two or three small ones, or one large and one small unit. Either of the latter arrangements will give you greater flexibility in the number of people you can serve and the variety of foods you can barbecue at one time.

If you plan to buy an electric motor for spit barbecuing, you must have an electrical outlet on the patio or a heavy duty extension cord.

Folks who like to do their outdoor cooking away from home—on the beach and picnic grounds or in the woods —will prefer smaller, portable units, the kind you can carry in the trunk of the car.

Examine the unit to see that it is well constructed. Here are a few pointers to keep in mind:

Chrome-plated grills give longer service than lightweight, nickel-plated wire grills. Closely spaced rods on the grill are an advantage too. Food is easier to manage and is less apt to fall through onto the coals.

Heavy gauge metals and cast iron give better service than lighter metals. They won't warp from the heat.

You have better control of the fire and cooking process if there is some way of ventilating the fire.

A mechanism for controlling the distance between the fire and the food is important too. Whatever the mechanism—screw-type, ratchet-type or just plain lugs for supporting the fire pan—be sure it is easy to operate.

Study the features and advantages of various units and equipment shown on the following pages, then pay your money and take your choice.

BARBECUE UNITS

Bucket Broilers

Lightweight, these units have a bale handle and usually have openings in the lower part for ventilating the fire. Cooking capacity is rather small for grilling. Using a large pan you can cook for a larger group. They are easy to pack in the car for beach and picnic use.

Hibachis or Oriental Cookers

These cookers are sturdily made of cast iron and always have a damper for fire control. Cooking surface is slightly larger than on most bucket broilers. They are excellent for beach and picnic use.

Vertical Grills

These units have one or two fire-boxes which are filled from the top with charcoal. Food is placed in racks which hang at the sides for grilling. Some units of this kind can also be used for pot and pan cooking.

Folding Grills

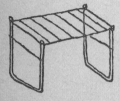

Sizes of folding grills and materials used varies. The simplest are made with a wire grid and legs which are stuck into the ground to make the unit rigid; the fire is built on the ground. The grid of another model is made of expanded metal and a sheet metal pan holds the briquets. Sturdier units made of cast iron have an arrangement to adjust distance between the grid and coals.

Folding grills are excellent for beach, park and picnic use.

Braziers

Braziers range in size from 12 to 30 inches in diameter and are supported on three legs.

Small units are made of sheet metal, grills are non-adjustable and bowls are shallow. About a foot high, they are convenient to use on a picnic table.

Larger units are made of cast iron, have deep bowls and a mechanism to adjust the distance of the grill from the fire. They stand at a good working height. These units are equipped with wheels. Some can be taken apart and transported in the car to the beach or picnic grounds.

Wagons, Carts or Tables

These square or rectangular units come in a range of sizes. These stand at worktable height and are on wheels which make them easy to move. Materials used and construction varies greatly. Most of these units have either an adjustable fire pan or grill and many have permanently attached hoods.

Kettle Units

A kettle unit resembles a large kettle on legs. It has a dome cover and several dampers for fire control. There are two grills in the kettle. The lower one holds the charcoal; the second grill, several inches higher, is for the food. These units range in diameter from 15 to 36 inches.

Permanently Built Units

If the chef is also a handyman, he may prefer to build his own unit on the patio. It can be simple or elaborate according to the dictates of his energy and his purse. There are many good books which have plans and complete information for building. See page 159 for books to consult.

Camp Stoves

An entirely separate class of units is the camp stove. These come in 1-, 2- and 3-burner units and require a specific liquid, gas or canned heat for which they are built. Popular with hunters and fishermen, they are suitable only for pot and pan cooking.

HOODS AND WINDSHIELDS

For larger braziers and wagon units, a hood or wind-shield is a good addition. It may be permanently at-tached or detachable. When you purchase the unit, if you don't have the money to invest in a unit complete with a hood, buy the unit now and the hood later.

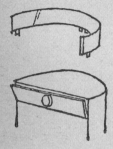

A hood or windshield saves fuel and gives better control of heat while cooking. A hood is more efficient than a windshield for it shields the top and sides.

Some hoods have warming ovens convenient for heating breads and keeping cooked foods hot.

SPITS AND MOTORS

Unless you have all the patience in the world, you'll want a motor-driven spit. Without one you must turn the roast every five minutes during the entire cooking process. Two types of motors are available, one operates on elec-tricity, the other on batteries.

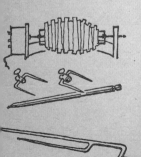

You have best results if your spit is a part of the hood unit. How-ever, some spits operate with a windshield; others are suspended from metal supports at either side of the unit.

Spit forks for the rods should be sturdily made. Most spit rods and spit forks are made separate-ly. A few rods however, have one fork permanently attached and one separate.

WHAT MAKES A GOOD FIRE

No matter what kind of equipment you use, a good fire is essential for successful barbecuing. And a good fire depends on many things—the fuel used, the ventilation of the fire as you light it, the way in which you light the fire and the arrangement of the briquets for the actual cooking. As the food cooks other conditions must be taken into consideration such as distance of food from the fire and flame-up.

FUELS TO USE

The fuel you use depends on several things—the kind of barbecue unit you have, the type of cooking you plan to do and personal preference. Whatever the fuel, be sure you have enough to complete the cooking job at hand.

Because of the popularity of charcoal and its general availability, the barbecue recipes in this book have been based on the use of charcoal briquets. Time required for cooking or distance from the heat may vary if other fuels are used but any difference will be slight.

Charcoal

This handy fuel comes in lump and briquet form and is packed in 5-, 10- and 20-pound bags. In addition, briquets are available in 2-pound self-starting boxes. These packages are particularly convenient for they are tightly sealed, so are clean to handle, store and use.

Lump charcoal catches fire more quickly, is a little cheaper, burns faster and has more charcoal aroma. Briquets, although slower to take fire, provide longer, steadier, hotter heat and will not spark while burning. A quart of lump charcoal is equal to about 6 briquets. Both kinds of charcoal are available in food stores, hardware stores and at many state parks, and picnic areas.

Wood

Where you cook, what you cook and personal preference play a big part in selection of the wood you burn. Wood is fine for fires built on the ground or rocks, in permanently built units and for some kinds of pit barbecuing. For a fire you need three types of wood—fine twigs, pieces of bark or wood shavings for tinder, larger twigs for kindling and logs for the real fire.

Soft woods—pine, spruce, cedars and gray birch— burn quickly so are good for starting the fire. Hardwoods—oak, yellow birch, maple, ash and mesquite to name a few are compact, firm and feel heavy in the hand. These woods burn more slowly and yield hotter coals than soft woods so are better for actual cooking.

Avoid woods that crumble. They are rotten and smolder without providing heat. If you are in the woods and the weather is damp use dead branches from trees rather than wood from the ground.

Bottled Gas, Liquid and Canned Fuels

Camp stoves are in high favor with some outdoor cooks. Each requires a specific fuel for which it was built. Manufacturer's instructions with the stove tell what fuel to use and how to use it. Fuels include white gas, available at boat supply stores and filling stations, wood alcohol, canned heat and bottled gas and liquid fuels available at camp supply and hardware stores.

VENTILATION FOR THE FIRE

Fire must have ample ventilation to start as well as to continue to burn. An expert fire tender knows how to handle his equipment to get the correct ventilation.

Take Advantage of the Wind

When you build a fire on the beach or in the woods on the ground, select a spot where you have a gentle breeze. Be sure, of course, that the spot is at a safe distance from trees, shrubs and grass that could catch fire.

Units, such as collapsible grills, having no air vents should be placed to take advantage of the breeze.

Hoods

A hood or windshield on a unit is an excellent aid in fire starting. Set the unit with the open side toward the breeze. Then, turn it as necessary, while food is cooking to control cooking speed.

Damper Control

Some units such as wagons, hibachis and kettle-type have a damper to control the flow of air through the unit around the fire. When you start the fire, open the damper and place the unit, if possible, so wind blows into the opening. After the fire is lighted, you can close the damper to control the speed of burning.

Gravel Bed for Braziers

When using a brazier, for best results, fill the bowl with a porous material such as pea gravel, cinders, sand or vermiculite. Whichever material you use, bring it out to the edge of the bowl and keep the bed level. In addition to providing ventilation for the fire, this bed helps reflect heat and protects the bowl for longer wear. After several barbecues, the air spaces will become clogged with charcoal ash and fat drippings and, as a ventilator, the base may lose its efficiency. When this happens, replace the material. In the case of gravel, you can wash it in a pail of water, spread it out to thoroughly dry, then return it to the brazier.

TO START A CHARCOAL FIRE

We have come a long way from starting a fire by rubbing sticks together or using flint and steel. There are many fire starters now available to make the procedure an easy one. But no matter where you start your fire, the charcoal and the area where you build your fire, whether it's a fancy unit or a hole in the ground, must be dry.

Chemical Starters

There is a great variety of chemical starters to choose from: liquids to sprinkle, squirt or spray and waxes, pastes, flakes and sticks. When using any of these, make a pile of 12 to 15 briquets, apply the starter as directed by the manufacturer and light with a match.

Homemade Starters

If need be, you can start a fire with a paraffined milk carton—or even newspapers. To use the milk carton, cut off the top and cut a hole, 1-inch square, in the bottom. Fill the carton with charcoal; lay the carton on its side and light with a match.

Cape Cod logs also work fine as a starter. To make them, open up several sheets of newspaper; pile them on top of each other. Start at a corner and roll up diagonally toward the opposite corner; tie in a knot. Put 4 or 5 knots in a heap with charcoal on top and light with a match. These paper logs are bulky, so are not well-suited for use in a barbecue unit, but they are fine for building a fire on the sand or rocks.

Electric Starters

You might prefer using one of the electric starters now available. They have a fast-heating rod or surface and require a 115 to 120V outlet. Arrange briquets about two deep, keeping the top surface flat. Plug in the starter, then lay the starter on the briquets and allow it to remain until gray ash forms on the briquets touching the heating element. This usually take 5 to 7 minutes. Then, move the starter to a new area. Repeat, as necessary, until enough briquets are lighted.

FIRE ARRANGEMENT

Whatever starter or method of fire building you use, be sure to allow plenty of time. It takes from 15 to 45 minutes after you start the fire until it is ready for cooking. Small gray spots appear on the briquets when they are first lighted. These gray spots are ash which results from the burning and must spread until the briquets are entirely covered with gray. Not until then is the fire ready to use.

Arrangement of the briquets depends on the kind of unit you have and the food you are cooking. Look over the sketches below. Then, with fire tongs or a rake, arrange the briquets to suit your particular needs.

Use this arrangement for braziers, wagons, folding grills with large fire pan and for fires built on sandy surface for barbecuing with hand grills.

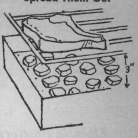

METHOD 1
Spread Them Out

Allow about a half inch space between briquets. Cover an area slightly larger than the area covered by the meat you are cooking. Grill steaks, chops, hamburgs, hot dogs, etc. about 3 inches above the fire.

Follow this arrangement for spit barbecuing in braziers or wagons with a hood. Following the contour of the unit at the back, pile briquets about 3 deep. The fire should extend beyond the meat on the spit.

METHOD 2
Pile Them Deep

Briquets, piled 3 or 4 deep, make a fine fire when using pans on hibachis, or bucket-type units. You may also need this type of fire in any unit where there is a great distance between the grill and the fire.

This arrangement is suitable for spit barbecuing on a brazier or wagon without a reflector, in kettle-type braziers and for pit barbecuing.

METHOD 3
Make A Ring

Make a circle of briquets around and slightly larger than the food to be cooked. Depending on whether you want a slow or very hot fire, you can space them closely, far apart, or even heap them slightly.

HEAT CONTROL—COOKING SPEED

Barbecuing is much more fun than cooking on even the most modern range with all its conveniences and although a barbecue unit has no thermostat, with a little experience, you can soon learn to judge how hot the fire is and what you must do to raise or lower the heat.

To Determine Heat of the Fire

Hold your hand over the coals at the same distance from the fire that the food will be while cooking. Now, count slowly—And 1, And 2, And 3 etc.—until you are forced to pull your hand away because of the heat.

A count of "And 1" means you have high heat, a count of "And 3" equals medium heat and a count of "And 5" equals low heat.

It stands to reason the greater the quantity of briquets, the hotter the fire, especially if they are very closely spaced or heaped high. To reduce the fire, spread the briquets over a greater area, remove some of the briquets, or cook the food at a greater distance from the fire. If you cook in a pan set directly on the coals, it may be necessary to spread the coals out until there is a space of 1½ to 2 inches between them.

The gray ash on briquets acts as an insulator and reduces the temperature of the fire. By tapping the briquets lightly with a rake or fire tongs, you knock the ash off and can utilize all the available heat. The ash will continue to accumulate as the briquets burn, so you may need to remove it periodically during the cooking period to maintain a fire of the right heat.

There are still other considerations beside the heat from briquets which affect cooking speed.

Air temperature is a big factor. The colder the temperature, the slower the cooking. On cold fall or winter days, allow a longer cooking time than in the summer.

Humidity is still another factor. When it is high, fire

is not only harder to start, but charcoal burns more slowly. And, on very humid days, the moisture in the air itself slows up the actual cooking. Charcoal and the gravel base on which the fire rests absorb moisture. It's a good idea to store the briquets in an airtight container to keep them as dry as possible.

Wind direction and speed must also be taken into account. A gentle breeze blowing into the fire is a good thing, but if too strong, the breeze not only carries away the heat, but also cools the food. If your unit has a built-in damper, you have no problem for you can control the amount of wind on your fire. A portable unit without a damper should be put in a spot where it is protected from the strong breezes, but with enough air to keep the fire burning properly. On beach or park parties, where you build an open fire on the ground, you may have to use your ingenuity to construct a windbreak to protect it from strong wind.

The temperature of the meat at the time you start barbecuing is an important factor. The colder the meat the longer it takes to cook. Always bring meat to room temperature before you start barbecuing.

A hood or windshield on a unit helps utilize all the heat from the fire. It acts as a windbreak protecting food from winds and reflects heat from the fire.

Flame-Up and What to Do About It

As meat cooks fat drips from it. When the fat strikes the hot briquets, you may have a good-sized flame to cope with. Some of this can be prevented by cutting excess fat from the meat before you start cooking. But even with trimming, there will be some dripping.

Spacing briquets over the gravel base when grilling on a brazier helps prevent flame-up. As fat drips it is absorbed by the gravel. A drip pan under the roast on a spit prevents fat from falling on the coals.

However, even with these precautions you may have some difficulty on grills and spits and you most certainly will have flame-up when the meat is cooked over a solid bed of coals. To quench the flame, squirt a little water on the coals. For this use a water pistol, a bottle with a sprinkler top or a basting tube—the kind made of glass with a rubber squeeze bulb attached. But, use the water cautiously. Too much water can reduce the temperature of your fire so much that cooking speed will be reduced.

SMOKING AND OTHER FLAVOR HELPS

Just as charcoal imparts its own distinctive flavor to the food cooked over it, specially selected woods also give food wonderful woodsy flavor. Hickory is the most readily obtainable wood but, apple, lemon, orange and hard maple are a few of the others sought by those who make a specialty of smoking. There are several methods by which you add wood flavors—hot smoking, cold smoking or if you like, use bottled seasoning.

Hot Hickory Smoking

Hot smoking takes place quickly during the normal cooking period. In addition to logs use hickory chips, flakes, or sawdust. They come in 2- and 5-pound bags or boxes and impart a fine flavor to food if properly used. This is the method used by the backyard chef, whose barbecue unit is too small for a wood fire, or for the city dweller who has trouble getting hickory wood.

  Chips must be put in water until thoroughly soaked. They are then placed on the burning charcoal fire. There is a difference of opinion about how fast the chips should burn.

  Some manufacturers recommend that you place the chips at the edge of the fire so they burn slowly without flaming. If they flame, remove them with tongs and douse the chips in water. Other manufacturers recommend putting the chips on a very hot fire so they ignite quickly. Meat is seared in the flames from the chips. Then the chips are pushed aside. Our advice is that you try both ways to see which suits your taste best.

To use the sawdust, it should be dampened, pressed into balls and placed on the charcoal fire, using tongs or a shovel. As the balls of sawdust char, replace them with fresh ones.

Wood flakes, to produce the best results, must also be dampened before scattering them over the fire.

These methods of getting special wood flavors in your food will satisfy even the gourmet, and they are mighty convenient to use.

Cold Hickory Smoking

This smoking process is accomplished in a specially constructed smoker or oven at a temperature of about 100°. It takes from 2 to 18 hours depending on the kind of food you smoke and the amount of flavor you want. For information about this type of smoker, we suggest you consult a dealer who handles this equipment. Or, if you are building your own unit, you might want to incorporate a smoke oven in it.

Other Flavor Helps

If you like a stronger charcoal flavor than you get from the charcoal fire, you might try smoke seasoned salt in place of regular salt. Liquid smoke rubbed onto meat before cooking is another way to increase smoke flavor. Either smoke salt or liquid smoke can be added to stews and mixtures cooked in a pan or sprinkled on vegetables before wrapping them in foil.

To get a combination of garlic and charcoal smoke flavor on a roast or steak, throw several cloves of garlic on the fire during the cooking proccss.

GRILL BARBECUING

Grilling—an age-old method of preparing meats—is one of the simplest and most popular forms of outdoor cooking. Whether your equipment is just a hand grill, a bucket broiler or a deluxe wagon unit, there's an endless variety of foods you can grill—not only meat, poultry and fish but fruits and vegetables too! Meat, poultry and fish recipes are on pages 24 to 42. Recipes for grilling fruits and vegetables are on pages 108 to 114.

And, remember, you can grill the inexpensive and less tender cuts of meats such as beef round steak as well as the more choice cuts. Tenderize them by scoring, pounding, using a marinade or commercial tenderizing agent as instructed in the individual recipes.

A Guide to Grilling

1. Have food at room temperature before barbecuing.

2. Be sure all briquets are coated with gray ash before starting to grill barbecue.

3. Arrange your ash-coated briquets according to either Method 1 or Method 2 as described on page 17. Have fire cover an area slightly larger than the food to be barbecued.

4. Always knock any gray ash off the briquets before putting your food on the grill.

22

5. When grilling lean meats, first rub the grill with a piece of fat or cooking oil to prevent meat from sticking.

6. Judging the heat of the fire is most important. In general, cook steaks and chops over a medium hot fire for the greater part of the cooking period. Spareribs, chicken parts and lean meats require a slower fire. See directions for determining the amount of heat, page 18.

7. To sear meat, either place it very close to the briquets or have fire very hot at the beginning. Then, reduce the amount of fuel or move meat farther away from heat before continuing to cook.

8. Baste lean meats and poultry constantly during cooking to keep them moist and juicy.

9. In general steaks and chops are ready for turning when juices appear on the top surface.

10. Try smoking and seasoning aids as a special addition to any grill barbecuing.

Important:

The grilling instructions above are intended only as a guide. Differences in the construction of barbecue units make it impossible to give instructions in each recipe that will cover all types of units.

In order to provide uniform procedures to serve as a guide, instructions are based on the use of brazier and wagon-type units having adjustable grills or fireboxes; cooking times are based on the fire arranged according to Method I. For other type units or other fire arrangements procedures may need to be revised and cooking times adjusted accordingly.

STEAKS TO GRILL

For a crowd or a dinner just for two—steak, tender, juicy and charcoal-flavored, is always a barbecue treat.

Of course, the choicest cuts to barbecue are sirloin, porterhouse, T-bone, club, rib, whole beef tenderloin or individual filet mignon. But, you can also barbecue such cuts as flank or round steak by using a slightly different cooking and/or carving procedure. Read the tips below to guide you in selecting your steak.

Then, barbecue the steak following the general instructions for Sirloin Steak on page 26, taking into account the special recommendations below. Remember, barbecuing time varies according to the heat of the fire and thickness of the steak. Times are based upon the specified thickness of each steak.

Porterhouse Steak

This steak has a "T"-shaped bone with a large portion of tenderloin. Have it cut at least 1½ inches thick. Barbecue 9 to 13 minutes per side.

T-Bone Steak

A steak similar in shape to a Porterhouse but smaller. Have steaks cut at least 1½ inches thick. Barbecue 9 to 13 minutes per side.

Tenderloin or Fillet of Beef

This steak is a boneless cut, very tender and easy to serve. Satisfy everyone—serve rare, medium and well done sections from one piece of meat. Barbecue a whole tenderloin 15 to 18 minutes per side, turning once.

Club Steak

This steak is small and has little or no bone. Have it cut 1½ inches thick. Grill 6 to 10 minutes per side.

Flank Steak

This steak should be of top quality. Select one cut about ¾ inch thick and having a good portion of fat. Have meat man score it to cut fibers.

Do not sear, but barbecue steak 1½ to 2 inches from hot briquets about 5 to 6 minutes per side. Steak is most tender cooked rare. Serve steak, cut diagonally across the grain, in very thin slices.

Round Steak

This steak should have a generous edging of fat and be cut about 1 inch thick. To prepare this less tender cut marinate it, using one of the recipes from page 120. Do not sear it. Grill steak 3 inches above hot briquets, allowing about 12 minutes per side for rare-done.

Rib Steak

This steak has a single bone along one side and should be cut at least 1½ inches thick. Grill steak about 3 inches from the hot briquets about 10 minutes per side, turning just once.

SIRLOIN STEAK

Sirloin steak, cut 1½ to 2 inches thick
  (allow ¾ to 1 pound steak per serving)
Fat or cooking oil
Salt and pepper to taste

Early Preparation

Score fat edge. But, don't cut into meat or juices will
be lost.

To Grill   *Time: about 25 min.*

Arrange hot briquets for grill barbecuing. Rub grill
with a piece of fat, cut from the steak, or cooking oil.
Lay the steak on the grill. Sear steak close to the coals,
2 to 3 minutes. Then, cook meat over medium heat,
moving it about 3 inches from briquets. When the meat
juices begin to rise on the uncooked surface, turn steak
over and sear second side 2 to 3 minutes. Return meat
to medium heat position; cook until done as desired. To
determine rareness of steak, use a small sharp knife
and make a slit alongside the bone; note color of meat.
Remove steak from grill and season with salt and pepper.

A 2-inch steak cooked rare, requires about 10 to 15
minutes per side barbecued 3 inches from coals.

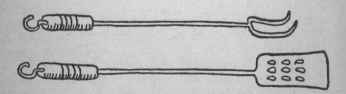

BURGER MAKING

Next time you wish you could do something different with that old standby hamburger, add pork or veal to the beef. Or, try lamb or corned beef burgers. Read the tips below. Then, prepare some of the recipes on pages 34 or 96 and make your own variations.

Select fresh meat and for tender burgers have it medium or coarsely ground. If meat is lean, have 2 ounces suet ground with each pound. For beef burgers buy round steak, chuck, flank or sirloin tip. For pork, veal or lamb burgers, buy shoulder or leg cuts.

Prepare burgers keeping these facts in mind:
For plain burgers, mix 1 teaspoon salt and a few grains pepper with each pound ground meat. One pound makes 4 large or 6 small patties. For tender burgers handle gently. Beef patties should be about ½ inch thick to be juicy. For medium-done hamburgers, grill over medium heat, about 15 minutes; turn once. Grill pork, veal or lamb until well done. Make patties thin, ¼ inch thick; grill about 15 minutes.

GRILLED SPARERIBS

**Loin spareribs with a generous amount of meat
(allow ¾ to 1 pound ribs per serving)
Sweet-Sour Basting Sauce (see page 126)**

Early Preparation

You will need long, slow grilling for spareribs as they
must be cooked to the well-done stage. So, be sure you
have low heat when starting to grill (see page 18). Prepare the Sweet-Sour Basting Sauce.

To Grill   *Approx. Time: 1 hour*

Arrange the hot briquets for grill barbecuing. Lay the
spareribs on the grill and cook slowly over low heat,
about 4 inches from briquets. Baste spareribs with
Sweet-Sour Basting Sauce every 2 to 3 minutes and turn
or they will dry out and burn. Barbecue ribs until well
done, or about 1 hour. Meat will shrink from the ends
of bones when done. To serve ribs, slice them apart
and serve with additional basting sauce or your favorite
barbecue sauce.

SPAREWICHES

| 2 sides spareribs | Apple Stuffing (see below) |
| (allow 4 ribs per serving) | Cooking oil |

Early Preparation

Cut each side of spareribs into 2-rib sections. Prepare Apple Stuffing. Place half the rib sections bone-side up; top with 2 to 3 tablespoons stuffing. Cover stuffing with a second rib section, meat-side up; tie with twine.

To Grill   *Approx. Time: 1 hour*

Arrange the hot briquets for grill barbecuing. Place spareribs on grill. Barbecue over low heat about 4 inches from coals until done, or about 1 hour. Brush with cooking oil and turn often. Remove twine; serve.

APPLE STUFFING

6 to 8 slices bacon, chopped	2 cups diced tart apples
½ cup finely chopped onion	2 tablespoons wine vinegar
½ cup brown sugar	1 cup soft bread cubes

Fry bacon in a skillet until crisp. Lift out bacon; reserve. Add onion, sugar, apple and vinegar to bacon fat. Cook and stir over medium heat, until onion is tender. Put bread cubes in a large bowl; add apple mixture. Toss to mix well. Makes about 2 cups.

PORK CHOPS

Buy rib or center-cut loin pork chops, cut 1 inch thick. Allow 2 chops per serving. Arrange hot briquets for grill barbecuing. Lay chops on grill; barbecue over low heat about 3 inches from briquets. Grill chops 30 to 40 minutes or until well done; turn just once.

LAMB FOR THE GRILL

You'll have added another specialty to your barbecue list when you serve your first charcoal grilled lamb chops or steaks.

When buying lamb chops select rib, center-cut, sirloin or shoulder cuts. Have them cut 1 to 2 inches thick. But, for really plump, juicy medium-done chops, have them cut 2 inches thick. Lamb steaks come from the leg and should be 1 inch thick to be most tender. But, remember, no matter which you buy, lamb chops or steaks, they are best served straight from the grill!

GRILLED LAMB STEAKS

Select shoulder lamb steaks, cut 1 inch thick. Allow 1 steak per serving. Melt some red currant jelly in a saucepan over low heat and set aside.

Arrange hot briquets for grill barbecuing. Grill steaks over medium heat until juices rise on uncooked surface. Turn steaks over and barbecue until almost done. Brush steaks several times with melted jelly during the last few minutes of barbecuing. When done, remove steaks from grill; season with salt and pepper.

Allow 12 minutes per side for medium-done steaks barbecued 3 inches from briquets.

KIDNEY LAMB CHOPS

Buy kidney lamb chops, cut 2 inches thick. Allow 1 chop per serving.

Arrange hot briquets for grill barbecuing. Sear chops on grill, close to the coals, 2 to 3 minutes. Then, barbecue meat about 12 minutes over medium heat, moving it about 3 inches from coals. Turn chops and sear second side 2 minutes. Return meat to medium heat position; cook until done. Season with salt and pepper. Chops cooked medium-done require about 15 minutes per side barbecued 3 inches from coals.

MINTED LAMB CHOPS

Lamb chops, cut 1 to 2 inches thick
(allow 1 to 2 chops per serving)
Mint Marinade (see below)
Salt and pepper to taste

Early Preparation

Marinate the lamb chops in Mint Marinade at room temperature for 1 to 2 hours. Lift chops out of marinade just before barbecuing. Save remaining marinade; use to baste chops during barbecuing.

To Grill   *Approx. Time: 25 to 30 min.*

Arrange hot briquets for grill barbecuing. Lay chops on grill and barbecue over medium heat, about 15 minutes. Turn chops and continue to barbecue until done as desired. To determine rareness of chops, use a small, sharp knife and make a slit alongside the bone; note color of meat. Medium-done chops should have just a very slight pink cast and juices running freely.

A 1½-inch chop grilled 3 inches from the briquets takes about 25 minutes total time to cook medium-done. Chops grilled well-done take about 30 minutes.

MINT MARINADE

Combine *1 cup prepared mint sauce and ⅔ cup cooking oil.* Pour over meat. Cover and let stand at room temperature about 2 hours, turning once. Makes enough to marinate 6 to 8 chops.

SHORT RIBS IN RUM

Buy beef short ribs. Have meat man cut ribs into pieces, about 2 inches square. Allow about 1 pound of short ribs per serving. Prepare Rum Marinade (see below).

Lay the short ribs in the marinade and marinate 4 hours at room temperature, turning occasionally. Or, cover container tightly and refrigerate ribs overnight. Just before barbecuing, drain ribs on paper towels. Reserve remaining marinade to use for basting.

Arrange the hot briquets for grill barbecuing. Place ribs on the grill. Barbecue ribs over medium heat, turning frequently, until done or 30 to 45 minutes.

Short ribs barbecued 3 inches from the briquets will take about 30 to 45 minutes.

RUM MARINADE

½ cup rum	1 teaspoon dry mustard
¼ cup soy sauce	1 tablespoon molasses
¼ cup canned pineapple juice	2 teaspoons ginger
1 to 2 tablespoons lemon juice	1 clove garlic, crushed
	½ teaspoon pepper

Combine all ingredients in a glass or enamel container; stir to mix well. Or, put marinade in a pint-size, screw-top jar; cover jar and shake. Store marinade in the refrigerator until ready to use. Makes about 1 cup.

SALT COATED CHUCK STEAK

Buy a chuck steak cut 3 inches thick. Crush several cloves of garlic. Spread crushed garlic over both sides of steak. Brush meat with cooking oil. Then, spread some prepared mustard on all sides of the steak and pour enough coarse (kosher) salt on top to cover it com-

pletely. The salt will form a crust around the meat.
Let steak stand in this crust about ½ hour or longer
for a more salty flavor.

Arrange briquets for grill barbecuing. Lay salt-coated
steak directly on the coals and barbecue, turning once.
A 3-inch chuck roast barbecued medium-done requires
25 minutes per side. For a steak cooked rare, barbecue
about 20 minutes per side.

To serve, chop salt crust off steak and slice the meat
across the grain.

STUFFED VEAL BIRDS

8 veal cutlets, sliced about ⅛ inch thick
(allow 1 cutlet per serving)
8 ounces liver sausage
1 egg, slightly beaten
2 tablespoons minced celery
1 tablespoon minced parsley
1 tablespoon minced green pepper
Cooking oil

Early Preparation

Have meat man flatten veal cutlets.

Put liver sausage into a bowl and mash with a fork.
Add egg, celery, parsley and green pepper; mix thoroughly. Put about 2 tablespoons liver mixture on each
cutlet; spread mixture evenly over slice. Roll each cutlet up from the narrow end like a jelly roll and secure
with a metal skewer; brush with cooking oil.

To Grill   *Approx. Time: 25 to 30 min.*

Arrange hot briquets for grill barbecuing. Place veal
rolls on grill and barbecue close to coals until well done,
turning and basting often with more oil.

Veal rolls barbecued 1 inch from hot briquets will
take about 25-30 minutes.

LAMBFURTERS

2 pounds ground lamb shoulder (allow ¼ pound per serving)	¾ teaspoon salt
3 tablespoons chopped parsley	¼ teaspoon pepper
¼ cup fine dry bread crumbs	⅓ cup pine nuts
1 clove garlic, crushed	2 eggs, slightly beaten
	8 frankfurter buns

Early Preparation

Combine lamb and next 7 ingredients. Shape mixture into 8 "fingers" the length of frankfurter buns.

To Grill   *Approx. Time: 15 min.*

Arrange briquets for grill barbecuing. Put lambfurters on grill; barbecue over medium heat until well done, turning frequently. Lambfurters barbecued 3 inches from the briquets will take about 15 minutes.

MIXED UP BURGERS

Buy *½ pound ground beef and ¼ pound each, ground veal and pork*. Allow ¼ pound meat per serving. Combine beef, veal and pork with *1 tablespoon minced onion, 1 teaspoon salt* and *⅛ teaspoon rosemary*. Shape meat into thin patties. Arrange hot briquets for grill barbecuing. Grill patties over medium heat until well done; turn often. Burgers cooked 3 inches from the hot briquets take about 20 minutes.

O'BRIEN'S SPECIAL

Use canned corned beef hash or your favorite hash recipe; shape into patties. Wrap sliced bacon around patties; secure with wooden picks. Grill patties close to coals until browned and hot; turn once.

CUBE STEAK SANDWICHES

Buy thinly sliced cube steak. Allow 2 cube steaks per serving. If desired, marinate the steaks several hours in one of the marinades from page 120. Drain steaks well before barbecuing.

Arrange hot briquets for grill barbecuing. Place steaks on grill, close to briquets. Barbecue steaks about 15 minutes, turning once to brown evenly. Season with salt and pepper and serve on hot, buttered toast.

CUBE STEAK QUICKIES

Buy thinly sliced cube steaks. Allow 2 steaks per serving. Combine equal parts of chopped bologna and pickle relish. Spread 2 to 3 tablespoons bologna mixture on each steak. Roll up steaks like jelly rolls; secure with wooden picks and brush with cooking oil.

Arrange hot briquets for grill barbecuing. Place rolls on grill over medium heat. Barbecue steaks until done, turning frequently to cook and brown evenly.

Steak rolls barbecued 3 inches from the hot briquets will take 15 to 20 minutes.

BEEF ROLLS

Use *8 thinly sliced cube steaks* and *8 slices bacon.* Two steaks and 2 slices bacon makes one serving. Prepare *1 cup packaged bread stuffing.* Spread 2 tablespoons of the stuffing on each steak and roll up like a jelly roll. Then, wrap each roll in a slice of bacon. Secure rolls with wooden picks.

Barbecue rolls on grill over medium heat, turning frequently. Rolls are cooked when bacon is crisp and meat is rare-to medium-done. Rolls barbecued 3 inches from the hot briquets will take about 20 minutes.

HOT DOGS AND SAUSAGES

Frankfurters and sausages are truly foods of convenience and are adaptable to most any kind of equipment. Hot dogs need only to be heated through; sausages with pork require longer cooking. Recipes for this popular barbecue fare are below and on page 95.

BARBECUED SAUSAGES

Buy pork sausage links, allowing 4 sausages per serving. Put sausages on grill over medium heat; barbecue until well-done, turning often to cook evenly. Sausages grilled 3 inches from coals take 20 to 30 minutes.

FRANKS IN SILVER

2 cups minced frankfurters
¼ cup grated processed American cheese
1½ teaspoons prepared mustard
2 hard-cooked eggs, chopped
1 teaspoon Worcestershire sauce
2 tablespoons pickle relish
¼ teaspoon garlic salt
2 tablespoons mayonnaise
¼ cup chili sauce
8 to 10 frankfurter buns

Early Preparation

Combine minced frankfurters and next 8 ingredients; stir to mix well. Hollow out centers of the buns. Fill buns with frankfurter mixture and close. Wrap buns securely in aluminum foil.

To Grill   *Approx. Time: 15 to 20 min.*

Arrange hot briquets for grill barbecuing. Put wrapped buns on grill, close to coals. Grill buns 15 to 20 minutes or until filling is heated; turn often. Makes 8 to 10 servings.

POULTRY FOR THE GRILL

Young birds—broilers or fryers—are a "must" when grilled over charcoal. Select the same kind of poultry you buy for oven broiling or frying. On the basis of ready-to-cook weight, chickens should weigh from 1½ to 2½ pounds; duckling from 3½ to 4½ pounds and turkeys about 4 pounds. Halve or quarter chickens and ducks; turkeys are best quartered. If the birds are frozen, defrost them before you start to cook.

BARBECUED CHICKEN HALVES

1½- to 2½-pound ready-to-cook, broiler-fryer chickens, halved (allow ½ chicken per serving)
Easy Basting Sauce (see below)

Early Preparation

Wash chicken thoroughly. Prepare Easy Basting Sauce recipe. Brush chicken with sauce.

To Grill   *Approx. Time: 25 to 30 min.*

Arrange hot briquets for grill barbecuing. Lay chicken on grill close to coals; sear both sides 2 to 3 minutes. Then, cook chicken over medium heat moving it about 3 inches from the briquets. Brush chicken with more sauce and turn often, barbecue until done, or 25 to 35 minutes depending on size.

EASY BASTING SAUCE

Put ⅓ *cup wine vinegar*, ⅓ *cup fresh lemon juice* and ⅓ *cup salad oil* in a screw-top jar. Add ½ *teaspoon soy sauce* and *pepper* and *salt* to taste. Cover jar and shake to mix well. Makes 1 cup.

HERBED CHICKEN BREASTS

4 chicken breasts, split (allow 1 breast per serving)
¼ cup butter or margarine, softened
¼ cup minced parsley
2 tablespoons minced onion
¼ teaspoon thyme
Sour cream, if desired

Early Preparation

Put the butter into a small bowl. Add the parsley, onion and thyme; mix well and set aside.

Wash the chicken breasts and pat dry with paper towels. Use a small, sharp knife to make pockets in the thickest part of the breasts. (Cut the slits parallel to the skin and large enough to hold 1 or 2 teaspoons of the butter mixture.) Fill each pocket with a spoonful of butter mixture; close with wooden picks.

To Grill   *Approx. Time: 15 min.*

Arrange hot briquets for grill barbecuing. Place stuffed breasts, skin-side down on the grill close to briquets. Barbecue chicken until done or about 15 minutes; turn once. If desired, brush chicken with some sour cream during the last few minutes of barbecuing.

BARBECUED DUCKLING

Select ready-to-cook duckling, weighing 3 to 5 pounds. Allow about ¼ duckling per serving. Have meat man quarter the birds. If duckling is frozen, thaw it completely; then, wash and dry thoroughly. Brush duckling with cooking oil. Arrange hot briquets for grill barbecuing. Put duckling on grill, cut-side down; barbecue over medium heat, turning frequently, until done as desired. Duckling, barbecued 3 inches from the hot briquets, takes 45 minutes to 1 hour.

FISH STEAKS

Buy salmon, halibut or haddock fish steaks, cut 1 inch thick. Allow about 1 pound per serving. Thaw frozen fish completely before barbecuing. For added flavor, prepare the Herb Marinade below. Marinate fish steaks for about ½ hour before barbecuing, then, drain well. Brush steaks with cooking oil.

Arrange hot briquets for grill barbecuing. Place steaks on grill over medium heat and barbecue about 12 minutes, turning once.

Fish steaks, barbecued 3 inches from the hot briquets take about 12 minutes.

HERB MARINADE

Combine *1 or 2 bay leaves, ½ teaspoon thyme* and *1 cup wine vinegar* in a small saucepan; heat to blend flavors. Cool the marinade. Put fish into a shallow dish and pour marinade over fish. Cover dish and let stand about ½ hour. Drain fish before barbecuing.

SMALL WHOLE FISH

Select small, whole fish such as butterfish, bluefish, snappers and trout. Allow 2 small fish per serving. Have fish cleaned and if desired, have the head removed. Wash fish thoroughly and pat dry with paper towels.

Make a thin paste of equal parts of flour and cooking oil. Season to taste with salt and pepper. Coat each fish with the mixture.

Arrange hot briquets for grill barbecuing. Place fish on grill over medium heat. Barbecue 6 to 8 minutes; turn fish once, grasping by head with tongs.

Fish barbecued 3 inches from the hot briquets takes 6 to 8 minutes.

CHARCOAL BROILED LOBSTERS

Buy 1- to 1½-pound lobsters. Have them split length-wise and cleaned. Allow 1 lobster per serving. Open lobsters as flat as possible. Prepare Drawn Butter (see recipe below); keep hot.

Arrange hot briquets for grill barbecuing. Lay lobsters, shell-side down, on grill; barbecue over medium heat about 15 minutes, brushing often with melted butter. Turn lobsters; grill about 5 minutes more. Shell is red when done. Serve with Drawn Butter. Lobsters grilled 3 inches from coals take about 20 minutes.

DRAWN BUTTER

½ cup butter	1½ teaspoons lemon juice
2 tablespoons flour	1 cup hot water

Melt ¼ cup of the butter in a saucepan; mix in flour, lemon juice and water and bring to a boil, stirring constantly. Cook and stir 5 minutes. Remove from heat; stir in remaining butter. If desired, add a few drops of yellow food coloring. Makes 1½ cups.

BARBECUED LOBSTER TAILS

Buy lobster tails weighing about ½ pound each. Allow 1 tail per serving. Slit undershells of tails, lengthwise, with scissors to prevent curling; bend backwards to crack shells. Brush slit-sides with melted butter.

Arrange hot briquets for grill barbecuing. Put tails, shell-side down, on grill; barbecue over medium heat about 15 minutes. Brush slit-sides with melted butter; turn. Grill about 3 minutes more or until done. Shell will be bright red when done. Tails grilled 3 inches from the coals take about 18 minutes.

HERB STUFFED RABBIT

2½-pound domestic rabbit, cut in parts
  (allow 2 rabbit parts per serving)
¼ cup softened butter or margarine
¼ teaspoon rosemary
Few drops wine vinegar
1 teaspoon chopped parsley

Early Preparation

If rabbit is frozen, thaw completely before barbecuing.
Combine the butter, rosemary, vinegar and parsley in a
small bowl; set aside. Wash rabbit parts; pat dry with
paper towels. Use a small, sharp knife to make a pocket
in the flesh of each piece of meat. Cut slits in meat
large enough to hold 1 or 2 teaspoons of the butter mixture. Fill each pocket with a spoonful of mixture; close
with wooden picks.

To Grill   *Approx. Time: 25 to 30 min.*

Arrange hot briquets for grill barbecuing. Put rabbit
on grill; barbecue over medium heat 25 to 30 minutes
or until done, turning once. Rabbit barbecued 3 inches
from the hot briquets takes 25 to 30 minutes.

VENISON STEAKS

Slice venison steaks at least 1 inch thick. Allow 1 steak
per serving. Brush steaks with melted bacon drippings
or cooking oil.
  Arrange hot briquets for grill barbecuing. Place steaks
on grill close to coals. Sear both sides of steaks 1 or 2
minutes. Then, continue to barbecue over medium heat,
moving steaks about 3 inches from the hot briquets.
Barbecue 5 to 10 minutes on each side for rare- or
medium-done steaks, brushing with bacon drippings before turning.

BARBECUED WILD DUCK

2- to 2½-pound wild duck, halved or quartered
  (allow 1 pound of duck per serving)
  Game Marinade (see below)

Early Preparation

Wash duck and pat dry with paper towels. Prepare
Game Marinade. Marinate the duck several hours at
room temperature or overnight in the refrigerator.
Drain the duck before barbecuing.

To Grill   *Approx. Time: 10 to 15 min.*

Arrange the hot briquets for grill barbecuing. Place duck
on grill close to coals; sear 1 or 2 minutes on each side.
Then, continue to barbecue the duck over medium heat,
moving it about 3 inches from the briquets. Brush the
duck frequently with the Game Marinade and turn often.
Barbecue 10 to 15 minutes or until done as desired.

Wild duck, halved or quartered, barbecued 3 inches
from the hot briquets takes 10 to 15 minutes depending on desired rareness.

GAME MARINADE

1 large onion, sliced	5 juniper berries
1 large carrot, shredded	¼ teaspoon thyme
1 tablespoon chopped parsley	¾ cup white vinegar
1¼ teaspoons salt	¾ cup dry vermouth
6 peppercorns	¾ cup cooking oil

Put all ingredients into a bowl; mix well. Put game into
a shallow glass or enamel container and pour marinade
on top. Marinate game about 5 hours at room temperature or overnight in the refrigerator. Makes about 2¼
cups marinade.

BARBECUING ON A SPIT

A motorized spit allows you the greatest amount of leisure time to spend with your guests or to relax as the food cooks. And the tantalizing fragrance, rich golden brown color and delicate flavor of meat, self-basted in its own juices makes it hard to beat!

Roasts, poultry and whole fish, spit barbecued, require very little attention once they are properly spitted over a well-built fire. And, don't forget, this kind of barbecuing also cuts your preparation and clean up time to a minimum.

For additional pleasure add a flat, rectangular spit basket to your equipment. Then, you can also spit barbecue such things as chops, steaks, chicken parts and small whole fish.

RULES FOR USING A SPIT

1. Know the capacity of your unit. When barbecuing large cuts of meat, check to be sure food will rotate freely and that the weight of the food will not strain the motor. If using a wagon or brazier unit, remove the grill. On braziers, lift out center post.

2. Build the fire according to one of the methods described on page 15.

3. Assemble necessary basic small equipment, such as spit rod, spit forks, pliers, barbecue thermometer, weight compensators and drip pan.

4. Follow the method best suited to the cut of meat when balancing it on spit. See pages 46 to 49. Or, if you wish to use a spit basket, see page 51.

5. Insert a barbecue thermometer in the meat when specified in the recipe.

6. Arrange the hot briquets as best suits the unit, using Method 2 or 3 (see page 17).

7. Attach the spit rod to the motor.

8. If necessary, place a drip pan under the meat. Turn on the motor.

9. Use fire controls recommended on page 18 and 19 for best results when barbecuing.

10. As food revolves on the spit, juices come to the surface and baste it. However, for additional flavor you may baste the food with a basting sauce, melted butter or margarine, cooking oil or the natural juices from the drip pan.

11. Barbecue sauces may also be used for basting but, apply only the last 10 minutes of barbecuing.

BALANCE ON THE SPIT

Aside from controlling the fire there is nothing as important as proper balance of the meat on the spit when spit barbecuing. Meats poorly balanced will cook and brown unevenly. Read the information below, then study the specific instructions that follow before putting the meat on the spit—you'll be glad you did!

Perfect balancing of meat means that the meat will rotate smoothly when put on a motor driven spit. If improperly balanced even the heaviest duty motor will operate under a strain and wear out quickly.

Tie or Truss the meat to make it as compact as possible. This is the first step towards proper balance. Be sure there are no dangling wings or flaps of meat. These will burn and cause improper balance.

Estimate the Center of Gravity of the piece of meat before inserting the spit rod. To do this, first estimate the location of any bones which may prevent insertion of the spit rod and judge where the area of greatest weight comes. Next, plan where to insert the spit rod so as to divide this weight equally between the opposite sides of the rod.

Insert the Spit Rod (with a spit fork in position near blunt or handle end) through the estimated center of gravity. There are various methods of doing this but only the simplest will be illustrated in the specific instructions that follow. Use a hammer to force rod through, if necessary. Then, slip another spit fork on rod and push meat to the center of rod. Insert spit forks into meat and tighten screws slightly.

Check Balance by rotating spit rod back and forth on palms of hands. When meat is properly balanced on the rod, it rotates evenly. Or, attach the spit rod to the motor, allowing it to rotate just long enough to check the motion; then remove it. If meat tips or rolls unevenly, either reposition the meat on the rod or attach and adjust weight compensators. Tighten fork screws securely with pliers. During cooking, fork screws may need an additional tightening and weight compensators may need adjusting to maintain balance.

Boned and Boneless Roasts

Good for: Roasts such as boned, rolled beef, veal, lamb, pork and ham.

Early Preparation: Have the meat man bone, roll and tie, at 1½ inch intervals, bone-in meats such as ribs of beef and leg of lamb. If the meat is lean, have it wrapped in suet, salt pork or bacon before tying.

When meats are to be stuffed, have the meat man bone and prepare the meat for rolling. Stuff the meat as directed in the individual recipe and roll up like a jelly roll. If necessary, fasten the meat roll with metal skewers to hold it firmly while tying with heavy twine. If the meat is lean, wrap it in suet, salt pork or bacon before tying. Then, tie the roll with heavy twine, crosswise, at 1½ inch intervals. Tie another piece of heavy twine, lengthwise, around the meat looping it through each of the crosswise ties to hold the ends of the meat more firmly in place.

To Put Meat on Spit: Insert the spit rod through the center of the roast as shown in the illustration at the left. Insert the spit forks into the ends of the meat. Then, center the meat on the spit rod and tighten the fork screws slightly. Check the roast for balance and tighten the spit fork screws with a pair of pliers.

Leg and Shoulder Roasts

Good for: Whole fresh or smoked ham, picnic, leg of lamb, etc.

Early Preparation: When barbecuing an entire ham, have the meat man cut the ham in half, diagonally, as shown in the illustration below. Meat will be easier to balance, cook faster and if smoked, will have more flavor.

When barbecuing either a whole or half leg of lamb, have the meat man saw off the bone about 3 inches from the small end of the leg.

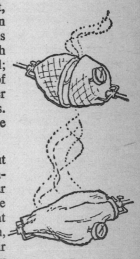

To Put Meat on Spit: To put an entire ham which has been cut in half on the rod, run the spit rod through each half of the meat, offsetting the butt end as shown in illustration at the right. This provides better balance. Push meat to the center of the spit rod; insert spit forks into both ends of meat. If necessary, use a hammer to insert the spit rod and forks. Check for balance. Tighten the spit forks with pliers.

When barbecuing whole, uncut legs, insert the spit rod, lengthwise, through the meat as near the center as possible. Insert the spit forks into each end of meat and check for balance. Then, tighten fork screws with a pair of pliers. These roasts, especially picnics, may be difficult to balance. The use of weight compensators are helpful when balancing these types of roasts.

Rib Roasts

Good for: Ribs of beef, pork loin, etc.

Early Preparation: Half a pork loin or less should be left in one piece when barbecuing. But, for better balance on the spit and faster cooking of an entire pork loin, cut the loin into 2 or 3 equal pieces. It is always necessary to use 2 spit forks to hold each piece of meat on the spit rod.

Two to seven ribs of beef may be barbecued at one time. Have the meat man remove the short ribs. For clearance on most units, rib bones should not be longer than 7 inches.

To Put Meat on Spit: Insert the spit rod in the meat, crosswise, to the bone. Be sure that the spit rod is through the center of gravity of the meat. Insert spit forks in the ends of the meat. Check the roast for balance. Tighten the fork screws with a pair of pliers.

Large Whole Fish

Early Preparation: Have the fish cleaned and the head removed. Lace the body cavity closed using some heavy twine and small metal skewers inserted at 1 inch intervals. (When the fish has been stuffed, lace the head cavity closed too.) Tie heavy twine around the body at 1 inch intervals.

To Put Fish on the Spit: Run the spit rod through the fish, lengthwise. Insert spit forks into the ends of the fish, bending the tines as necessary, to hold it. Tighten fork screws slightly. Check for balance. Tighten fork screws with a pair of pliers.

Poultry and Game

Good for: All birds such as chickens, turkey, domestic and wild duck, pheasant, etc.

Early Preparation: Have neck removed but not the neck skin. Bring neck skin over neck cavity. Turn under the edges of the skin; skewer to the back skin. Bring wings forward and flatten against the body between the thighs and breast of the bird. Loop heavy twine around the wings and neck end of the body several times to secure. Tie the legs and tail together.

To Put Poultry on the Spit: Run the spit rod through bird parallel to the backbone, bringing it out between tail and legs. Center bird on rod; insert spit forks in each end of bird. Tighten fork screws slightly. Check for balance and tighten fork screws.

If several small birds are to be barbecued, tie each one with twine. Dovetail the birds on the spit and for better balance, put the birds on the spit one breast-side up and the next breast-side down. Push birds together tightly; insert a spit fork in each end bird.

When several large birds are to be barbecued, use 2 spit forks for each bird.

The spit rod's capacity can be increased by putting small birds such as squabs on rod vertically (see page 85). Tie each bird as directed above. Insert rod, crosswise, through lower part of breast; alternate heads and tails. Use one spit fork for each two birds.

BARBECUE THERMOMETER

A meat thermometer is the best guide for determining when a roast is done. Use a barbecue thermometer or any unpainted, all metal meat thermometer.

Put the thermometer in the roast before attaching the spit rod to the motor. Insert the metal tip of the thermometer into the thickest part of the meat. But, to obtain a true reading remember these points:

1. Do not let the tip of thermometer touch the spit rod, or bone, or rest in fat. In birds such as chickens, capons and turkey the thickest part of the meat is in the body between the breast and thigh. For small or boney birds such as squab, Cornish hens and ducks, a thermometer is not practical.

2. Insert the thermometer at a slight angle to the spit rod so it will not fall out as meat revolves.

3. Check the clearance. Be sure the thermometer does not touch the briquets, drip pan or hood.

4. When meat is cooked remove the spit rod from unit, lift thermometer out of meat; slip meat off rod.

DRIP PAN

For most spit barbecuing, a drip pan is a must for catching the fat and juices which drop from the meat. These drippings are excellent for basting or for making sauces and gravies. A pan also prevents fats from falling on the fire, causing flame-up and excessive smoke.

For a drip pan you can use any shallow metal pan that is slightly longer than the meat to be barbecued. Or, make a drip pan from heavy duty aluminum foil.

To make a pan, use foil 18 inches wide. Tear off a

piece of foil about 5 inches longer than meat; fold in half, lengthwise. Next, make sides by turning up all 4 edges about 1½ inches; fold or mitre corners to seal.

Place the pan a little forward, but under meat before starting to barbecue. Be sure there are no coals under the pan to cause collected fats and juices to burn.

SPIT BASKET

Once you've used a spit basket to barbecue small pieces of meat, fish or poultry and, especially those which require long cooking, you'll wonder how you ever did without it! All meats need less attention in a basket than when grilled. Some recipes in the spit barbecuing section have been written for the spit basket but, you will discover many recipes from the grill section can also be adapted to a spit basket. Points to remember when you use the spit basket are listed below.

1. Always have the meat uniform in thickness.

2. Arrange the food in the basket as close together as possible. If you are barbecuing small whole fish, alternate the heads and tails. Food should lay flat.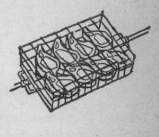

3. Fasten the cover in place over the food very securely to prevent the food from falling out or slipping to one side as it cooks.

4. When using a recipe from the grill section allow a little more time for the food to cook.

BEEF FOR ROASTING

Serve roast beef any time. No matter what roast you choose, a standing rib, a boned rolled roast, a tenderloin or a less expensive cut such as an eye of round—it will taste better barbecued!

For something different, add a subtle flavor to compliment the beef. Brush the meat with one of the basting sauces suggested in the chart on page 124, add a few hickory chips to the fire, or use one of the "Other Flavor Helps" from page 21. Everyone will want to know your secret. In addition to the beef recipes below others may be found on pages 53 and 54.

STANDING RIB ROAST OF BEEF

Standing rib roast of beef, 2 or more ribs
   (allow about ¾ pound per serving)
Cloves of garlic for fire, if desired

Early Preparation

Put the meat on the spit rod as directed for Rib Roasts on page 48. Insert a barbecue thermometer in meat.

To Spit Barbecue   *Time: 14 min. per lb.*

Arrange the hot briquets to give medium heat for spit barbecuing. Attach the spit rod to the unit and place a drip pan under the meat. Turn on the motor. Throw cloves of garlic on the fire.

The beef is cooking when the fat bubbles slightly and drips from the lowest point on the meat. Barbecue it until done as desired, allowing 12 to 15 minutes per pound. The barbecue thermometer should register 140° for rare, 160° for medium, or 170° for well-done beef.

When beef is done lift out thermometer and remove meat from the spit. Let meat stand about 10 minutes to firm up before carving. Carve and serve immediately.

ROLLED RIB ROAST

Buy a rolled rib roast of beef, weighing at least 4 pounds; allow ⅓ pound per serving. Put beef on spit as directed for Boned and Boneless Roasts on page 46.

Barbecue the beef allowing 12 to 15 minutes per pound. The thermometer should register 140° for rare, 160° for medium, or 170° for well-done beef. If desired, baste meat occasionally with Fiesta Sauce (see below). When meat is done, remove spit rod. Let meat stand 10 minutes to firm up and cut crosswise into slices. Serve any remaining sauce over the sliced beef.

FIESTA SAUCE

Melt ⅓ *cup butter or margarine* in a saucepan. Add ¾ *cup finely chopped onion;* cook over low heat until soft, but not brown. Slowly add and stir in ½ *cup white wine;* add *2 teaspoons salt.* Bring mixture to a boil and simmer 5 minutes; remove from heat. Add *2 table- spoons minced parsley.* Mix well. Makes about 1½ cups.

BARBECUED FILLET OF BEEF

A whole fillet or tenderloin of beef, about 4 pounds
  (all ⅓ to ½ pound per serving)
Cloves of garlic, if desired

Early Preparation

Cut several slits in the fillet of beef and insert cloves of garlic or, if desired, save garlic to throw on the fire later. Put the meat on the spit as directed for Boned and Boneless Roasts on page 46. Insert a barbecue thermometer in the thickest part of the fillet.

To Spit Barbecue   *Approx. Time: 45 min.*

Arrange the hot briquets to give medium heat for spit barbecuing. Attach the spit rod to the motor and place a drip pan under the meat. Turn on the motor. If cloves of garlic were not inserted in the meat, throw several cloves on the fire.

Barbecue the fillet about 45 minutes or until thermometer registers 140°. Since the fillet is uneven in thickness you can serve rare beef from the thick end, medium and well-done beef from the thinner end.

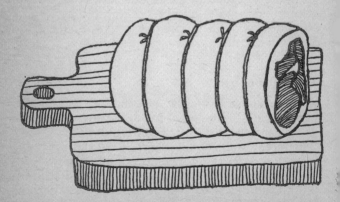

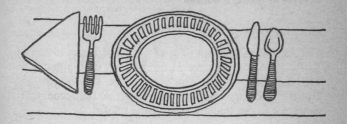

LEG OF LAMB

6- to 7-pound leg of lamb
    (allow ½ to ¾ pound meat per serving)
Cooking oil
¼ cup red currant or mint jelly, if desired

Early Preparation

Put the leg of lamb on the spit rod as directed for Leg and Shoulder Roasts on page 47. Insert a barbecue thermometer and brush lamb with cooking oil. Melt the jelly in a small saucepan and set aside.

To Spit Barbecue   *Time: 30 min. per lb.*

Arrange the hot briquets to give medium heat for spit barbecuing. Attach the spit rod to the motor and place a drip pan under the meat. Turn on the motor.

Barbecue lamb allowing about 30 minutes per pound for well-done meat. Thermometer should register 170° for medium and 180° for well-done meat. If desired, brush lamb frequently with the melted jelly during the last 10 to 15 minutes of barbecuing time. When lamb is done remove from spit; lift out thermometer.

HAM

Whether you select a whole ham, half ham, boned, rolled ham, picnic shoulder or smoked shoulder pork butt, keep in mind the following terms: "fully-cooked" or "ready-to-eat" and "cook-before-eating." The tag, wrapper or meat itself will bear one of these names.

Know the type of ham you are buying, it will be a guide to barbecuing time. If you are pressed for time, select a "fully-cooked" or "ready-to-eat" ham or picnic. These precooked meats need only to be heated through. They will take about 10 minutes per pound to barbecue. The barbecue thermometer should register 170° when the meat is done.

The "cook-before-eating" meats require a longer barbecuing period, about 25 minutes per pound. When cooking this type of meat, rely on the barbecue thermometer as your guide. It should register 190° when meat is done. If the ham has an artificial casing, be sure to remove it before putting the ham on the spit.

Ham is delicious when just plain barbecued but, when coated with one of the glazes or barbecue sauces on pages 128 or 130, it is superb!

56

BARBECUED HAM

8- to 10-pound ready-to-eat whole ham
  (allow ½ pound per serving)
Apricot Honey Glaze (see recipe below)

Early Preparation

Put ham on spit as directed for Leg and Shoulder Roasts
on page 47 and insert barbecue thermometer. Prepare
the glaze.

To Spit Barbecue   *Time: 10 min. per lb.*

Arrange hot briquets to give medium heat for spit barbecuing. Attach spit rod to unit; put a drip pan under
meat. Turn on motor. Barbecue meat allowing 10
minutes per pound or until thermometer registers 140°.
Brush meat with glaze during last 15 minutes of barbecuing.

APRICOT HONEY GLAZE

Combine *1 cup firmly packed brown sugar, ½ cup
honey and ¼ cup canned apricot nectar* in a saucepan.
Heat and stir until sugar dissolves. Makes 1½ cups.

BARBECUED PICNIC
(see pic. on page 56)

Select a ready-to-eat picnic or shoulder ham, weighing
at least 5 pounds. Allow ½ pound per serving. Put ham
on spit as directed for Leg and Shoulder Roasts on page
47. Insert a barbecue thermometer. Arrange hot briquets to give medium heat for spit barbecuing. Attach
spit rod to the unit; place a drip pan under meat. Turn
on motor. Barbecue ham allowing about 10 minutes
per pound or until thermometer registers 140°.

BARBECUED BONED ROLLED HAM

Buy a ready-to-eat boned, rolled ham. Allow ⅓ pound per serving. Remove casing from ham; then tie it with twine and put on the spit as directed for Boned and Boneless Roasts on page 46. Insert a barbecue thermometer.

Barbecue meat until thoroughly heated, allowing about 10 minutes per pound. Barbecue thermometer should register 170°. If desired, baste ham occasionally with Beer Basting Sauce (see below).

BEER BASTING SAUCE

½ cup flat beer
2 tablespoons vinegar
1 tablespoon Worcestershire
  sauce

⅓ cup firmly packed
  brown sugar
1 tablespoon lemon juice
⅔ cup chili sauce

2 tablespoons honey

Combine all ingredients in a saucepan. Heat and stir until sugar dissolves. Makes about 2 cups sauce.

BARBECUED PORK BUTT

Smoked pork butts, weighing 3 pounds each
  (allow about ⅓ pound per serving)

Early Preparation

Remove any casing on meat. Put meat on spit as directed for Boned and Boneless Roasts on Page 46.

To Spit Barbecue   *Approx. Time: 1¾ hours*

Arrange hot briquets to give medium heat for spit barbecuing. Attach spit to unit. Place a drip pan under the meat. Turn on the motor. Barbecue meat until done, allowing 35 minutes per pound.

PORK

Pork, properly barbecued over low to medium heat, is a meat fit for the most festive affair. Whether you select spareribs or suckling pig for the menu, pork must be thoroughly barbecued. The meat should be grayish-white inside with no trace of pink, but still juicy when cooked. Rely on a barbecue thermometer for large roasts. This is the best guide to well-cooked pork. When meat is done, thermometer should register 190°. For chops and spareribs, cut a slit near the bone to be sure pork is done.

For a flavor change insert slivers of garlic into the roast; brush the meat with one of the glazes from page 128, or just add a few smoke chips to the fire.

SMOKED PORK LOIN

Pork loin, weighing at least 3½ pounds
 (allow ¾ to 1 pound per serving)
Smoke chips for the fire

Early Preparation

Have meat man split the backbone between each rib. And, if the roast is large have it cut into 2 or 3 pieces for better balance on the spit. Prepare smoke chips as directed on the package.

Put roast on the spit rod as directed for Rib Roasts on page 48. Insert barbecue thermometer.

To Spit Barbecue   *Time: about 35 min. per lb.*

Arrange hot briquets to give medium heat for spit barbecuing. Put a few smoke chips on the coals. Attach spit to the unit. Put a drip pan under the meat; turn on motor. Replace chips as they burn during cooking.

Barbecue meat until done, allowing 30 to 35 minutes per pound. Barbecue thermometer should register 190°.

BARBECUED FRESH HAM

Buy a whole fresh ham, weighing 10 to 14 pounds. Allow ½ to ¾ pound per serving. For better balance and faster cooking, have meat man cut ham in half diagonally and put it on the spit as directed on page 47. Insert a barbecue thermometer in the meat.

Arrange hot briquets to give medium heat for spit barbecuing. Attach spit to unit. Put a drip pan under ham. Turn on motor. Barbecue meat until done, allowing 30 to 35 minutes per pound. Barbecue thermometer should register 190° when pork is done.

A 12-pound ham barbecued over medium heat takes about 6 hours to be thoroughly cooked.

BARBECUED DOUBLE PORK LOIN

Buy two pork loins. Have meat man bone and put the loins together fat side out; tie with twine at 1½ inch intervals. Boned roast should weigh a total of at least 5 pounds for barbecuing. Allow ½ pound per serving. Prepare Currant Glaze below. Put pork on spit as directed for Rib Roasts on page 48. Insert barbecue thermometer in meat.

Arrange hot briquets to give medium heat for spit barbecuing. Attach spit to unit. Place a drip pan under pork. Turn on motor. Barbecue meat until done, allowing about 20 minutes per pound. Thermometer should register 190°. Brush meat with Currant Glaze during the last 10 or 15 minutes of barbecuing time.

CURRANT GLAZE

Combine ¾ *cup currant jelly, 2 tablespoons vinegar* and *2 tablespoons prepared horse-radish* in a small bowl; beat well. Makes 1 cup.

STUFFED SHOULDER OF PORK

4 pounds boned, fresh shoulder of pork
 (allow about ⅓ pound meat per serving)
⅓ cup butter or margarine, melted
1 cup finely chopped celery
¼ cup finely chopped onion
3 cups soft bread crumbs
¼ cup chopped Brazil nuts
1 teaspoon salt
⅛ teaspoon black pepper
¼ teaspoon caraway seeds
1 egg, slightly beaten

Early Preparation

Have the meat man open the boned pork for rolling.
Melt the butter in a small skillet; add celery and onion.
Cook and stir until the celery is tender but not brown.
Remove from heat.

Combine the bread crumbs, nuts, salt, pepper and caraway seeds in a large bowl. Add butter-celery mixture
and egg to the bread mixture; toss to mix well.

Spread the bread mixture evenly over the cut surface
of the pork. Starting from the long side, roll up meat
like a jelly roll. Fasten meat with metal skewers and
then, tie with heavy twine.

Put rolled pork on the spit rod as directed for Boned
and Boneless Roasts on page 46. Insert a barbecue
thermometer in meat.

To Spit Barbecue   *Approx. Time: 2½ hours*

Arrange hot briquets to give meduim heat for spit barbecuing. Attach spit to unit. Place a drip pan under
pork; turn on motor.

Barbecue meat until done, allowing about 2½ hours
total time, or until thermometer registers 190°. Let
meat stand about 10 minutes after removing from spit
to allow it to firm up before carving. Remove the thermometer, skewers and twine before carving.

SPARERIBS ON A SPIT

Select meaty spareribs for barbecuing. Allow about 1 pound of ribs per serving. Prepare Oriental Spice Mixture, below. Put ribs into a shallow container. Rub both sides of ribs with spice mixture. Let stand several hours at room temperature. Drain ribs before putting on the spit rod. To put ribs on rod, run spit rod through center of rack starting at narrow end and lacing rod between bones. Lace second rack on the rod starting at the wide end; continue until all spareribs are on the spit rod. Insert the spit forks and tighten. Then, run several metal skewers through the ribs on outer edges to hold them securely.

Arrange hot briquets to give medium heat for spit barbecuing. Attach spit rod to unit. Put a drip pan under meat. Turn on motor. Barbecue about 45 minutes to 1 hour or until done. If desired, ribs may be brushed with one of the barbecue sauces from page 130 during last 10 or 15 minutes of barbecuing time.

ORIENTAL SPICE MIXTURE

Combine *¾ teaspoon turmeric, 2 teaspoons paprika, a few grains dry mustard, 2 tablespoons salt* and *1½ cups sugar*. Put it in a screw-top jar and shake vigorously to mix well. Makes 1½ cups.

RIBS IN A BASKET

Buy meaty spareribs. Allow about 1 pound per serving. Cut spareribs into serving-size pieces.

Assemble the spit basket according to manufacturer's directions. Arrange the spareribs in the spit basket (see page 51) and fasten the cover securely.

Arrange hot briquets to give medium heat for spit bar-

becuing. Attach the rod with the spit basket to the unit.
Place a drip pan under the basket and start the motor.
Barbecue the spareribs 45 to 60 minutes or until done.
If desired, serve one of the barbecue sauces from page
130 as a dip for the spareribs.

STUFFED CHOPS IN A BASKET

6 pork chops, center-cut or rib, cut 1¼ inches thick
 (allow 1 chop per serving)
2 cups soft bread crumbs
¼ cup melted butter or margarine
½ teaspoon savory
2 tablespoons minced onion
½ teaspoon salt
Pepper, to taste
¼ cup orange juice

Early Preparation

Have meat man cut pockets in the chops, or make a slit
with a small, sharp knife cutting from the fat side in
toward the bone.

Combine in a large bowl, the bread crumbs, butter,
savory, onion, salt, pepper and orange juice. Toss to mix
stuffing mixture well. Fill meat pockets with stuffing.
Fasten with wooden picks.

Assemble the spit basket according to manufacturer's
directions. Arrange the chops in the spit basket and
fasten the cover securely (see page 51).

To Spit Barbecue   *Approx. Time: 1¼ hours*

Arrange the hot briquets to give medium heat for spit
barbecuing. Attach the rod with the spit basket to the
unit. Place a drip pan under the basket; start motor.
Barbecue the chops 1 hour and 15 minutes or until
done, basting occasionally with pan drippings.

BARBECUED SUCKLING PIG

Keep the size of the barbecue unit in mind when you order a suckling pig. Most units 24 inches wide will accommodate a pig from 8 to 14 pounds; one 30 inches wide will accommodate a pig up to 20 pounds. If you wish to barbecue a larger suckling, you can remove the head and legs, but the roast won't look much like a pig.

Prepare the Roast Suckling Stuffing and the Suckling Sauce (see below); set aside. Wash pig inside and out with cold water and if necessary, remove any remaining tissues from body cavity. Dry pig well. Rub salt and pepper in the body cavity and fill with stuffing. Close the cavity by inserting small metal skewers at 1-inch intervals; then, lace tightly with twine.

Bring front legs of pig forward so feet are near the corners of mouth; tie legs securely with more twine. Bring hind feet forward almost as far as the forefeet and tie securely with twine. When pig is trussed it must be about 4 inches shorter than width of unit.

Put a spit fork in position on the blunt or handle end of the spit rod. Using a hammer, insert the rod through the pig. Slip another spit fork on rod; insert both forks in the pig and tighten slightly. Put a small block of wood in pig's mouth. Check for balance; use weight compensators if necessary. Tighten fork screws securely with a pair of pliers. Insert a barbecue thermometer in heaviest part of hind quarters. Brush the pig with some Suckling Sauce.

Pile the hot briquets for spit barbecuing as directed in Method 2 on page 17 and extend the briquets making a semicircle around the area where the butt end of the pig will be. Attach spit to unit; put a drip pan under pig. Turn on motor. Barbecue the pig over medium heat, basting often with more sauce and some of the pan drippings. Allow about 20 minutes per pound barbecuing time. The barbecue thermometer should register 190° when the pig is done. Reduce heat around head end of pig towards end of cooking period, if necessary. A 14-pound suckling takes about 5 hours.

When pig is done, place on a large platter. Remove thermometer, spit forks and rod, wooden block and strings which hold legs to body. Insert cherries in the eye sockets and a small red apple in the mouth.

ROAST SUCKLING STUFFING

½ cup butter	⅛ teaspoon pepper
1 cup pine nuts	½ to 1 teaspoon rosemary
2 medium-size onions, chopped	¼ cup chopped parsley
	5 to 6 cups dry bread crumbs
1 clove garlic, minced	½ cup sherry
1 teaspoon salt	½ cup water

Put a little of the butter in a large skillet. Add nuts; cook and stir over low heat until nuts are browned. Remove nuts from pan; set aside.

Melt remaining butter in skillet. Add onion and garlic; cook and stir until onion is soft. Combine nuts, salt and next 4 ingredients in a bowl; mix well. Add onion mixture. Sprinkle sherry and water on top. Toss to mix well. Enough to stuff a 15-pound suckling.

SUCKLING SAUCE

1 cup butter or margarine	1 tablespoon Worcestershire sauce
2½ cups water	
1 teaspoon dry mustard	2 teaspoons black pepper
2 tablespoons sugar	1 tablespoon paprika
2 teaspoons chili powder	¼ teaspoon cayenne pepper
¼ cup lemon juice	½ cup minced onion
1 clover garlic, minced	

Combine all ingredients in a saucepan. Bring mixture to boiling over high heat; reduce heat to low and simmer, covered, about 20 minutes. Makes about 3½ cups.

BARBECUED EYE OF ROUND

Beef eye of round, about 5 pounds
(allow about ⅓ pound per serving)
Tangy Barbecue Sauce (see page 133), if desired

Early Preparation

Have the meat man wrap beef in suet or salt pork and tie with heavy twine at 1½ inch intervals. Put meat on spit as directed for Boned and Boneless on page 46 and insert a barbecue thermometer. Prepare the barbecue sauce; double recipe for 4 to 5 pound roast.

To Spit Barbecue   *Time: about 10 min. per lb.*

Arrange the hot briquets to give medium heat for spit barbecuing. Attach the spit rod to the unit and place a drip pan under the beef. Turn on the motor.

Barbecue meat, allowing about 10 minutes per pound or until done as desired. The thermometer should register 150° for medium-rare beef. Brush meat with some of the sauce the last 10 to 15 minutes of barbecuing; serve remaining sauce with sliced beef.

EYE OF ROUND FOR A CROWD

For a crowd Barbecued Eye of Round makes delicious sandwiches. This solid meat is so easy to slice and there's little or no waste. Remember too, due to its shape, a heavier piece takes only a little longer to barbecue than a lighter weight piece.

A whole eye of round, weighing 10 pounds, can make as many as 75 sandwiches, if sliced on a machine. But, first let the cooked meat stand about 10 minutes to firm up. Then, before putting the meat on the slicer, cut it into several shorter lengths. Serve sliced beef in buns topped with your favorite barbecue sauce. Allow about 3 pints sauce for each 10 pounds of meat.

SHORT RIBS ON THE SPIT

Select a piece of meat with at least 3 ribs. Allow ¾ to 1 pound of short ribs for each serving. The ribs must be meaty and should measure 3 to 4 inches at the thick end. The bones should be from 4 to 6 inches long and they should not be cracked. When barbecuing 6 or more ribs have meat cut into 2 pieces. Marinate the meat, if desired, for several hours in one of the marinades suggested on page 120.

Put the meat on the spit rod with the rod at right angles to the rib bones. Insert the spit forks in the ends of each piece of the meat and test for balance. Tighten the spit forks and insert the thermometer in the thickest part of the meat.

Arrange hot briquets to give medium heat for spit barbecuing. Attach the spit to the unit. Put a drip pan under the meat; turn on the motor. Barbecue until done as desired, allowing about 25 minutes per pound. Time depends on total weight and thickness of meat. Thermometer should register 160° for medium-done ribs.

CHUCK IN A SPIT BASKET

Have meat man cut a top quality chuck steak 1 to 1½ inches thick. Allow ⅓ to ½ pound per serving.

Prepare one of the marinade recipes from page 120. Pour marinade over steak in a bowl. Let it stand several hours at room temperature; turn occasionally. Just before cooking drain steak; save remaining marinade.

Assemble the spit basket using manufacturer's directions. Lay steak in basket and fasten cover securely. Arrange coals to give medium heat for spit barbecuing. Attach rod with basket to unit. Place a drip pan under basket; start motor. Barbecue steak until done as desired; brush often with remaining marinade. Steak cut 1½ inches thick takes about 45 minutes to cook medium-done. Serve steak sliced across the grain.

HERBED VEAL SHOULDER

3- to 4-pound boned shoulder of veal
 (allow ⅓ pound meat per serving)
1 teaspoon salt
¼ teaspoon pepper
¼ teaspoon paprika
6 slices bacon
½ cup chopped parsley
½ teaspoon marjoram
1 tablespoon chopped mint, if desired
½ cup finely chopped onion
Cooking oil

Early Preparation

Have meat man prepare the boned veal so it can be rolled. Lay meat, cut-side up, on a wooden board. Sprinkle it with salt, pepper and paprika. Lay the bacon slices on top of veal; sprinkle with parsley, marjoram, mint and onion. Starting from the long side, roll up meat like a jelly roll. Fasten the meat with metal skewers and tie it with heavy twine at 1½ inch intervals.

Put rolled veal on spit rod as directed on page 46. Insert a barbecue thermometer in the meat. Brush meat with cooking oil.

To Spit Barbecue   *Time: about 35 min. per lb.*

Arrange the hot briquets to give medium heat for spit barbecuing. Attach the spit to the unit. Place a drip pan under the veal; turn on the motor.

Barbecue meat until done, allowing 35 minutes per pound. Brush it often with cooking oil. Thermometer should register 170° when meat is done. Meat should be grayish-white in color when cooked. Veal barbecued over medium heat takes 2 to 2½ hours.

When meat is done, lift out thermometer. Remove meat from spit and remove twine. Let meat stand about 10 minutes to firm up before carving.

ROLLED RUMP OF VEAL

Buy a *boned rolled rump of veal, weighing from 3 to 4 pounds* and ½ pound thinly sliced salt pork or bacon. Allow about ⅓ pound meat per serving. Wrap veal in slices of salt pork and tie with twine at 1-inch intervals to secure pork.

Put veal on the spit rod as directed for Boned and Boneless Roasts on page 46. Insert a barbecue thermometer in meat. Brush veal with *cooking oil*.

Arrange hot briquets to give medium heat for spit barbecuing. Attach the spit rod to the motor. Place a drip pan under the veal and turn on the motor.

Barbecue meat until done, allowing about 40 minutes per pound. Interior of meat will be grayish-white in color when done and the barbecue thermometer should register 170°. Brush veal occasionally with pan drippings during barbecuing. Let meat stand about 10 minutes to firm up before carving.

LEG OF VEAL

Select a leg of veal, weighing at least 4 pounds. Allow about ⅓ pound per serving. Have meat man wrap salt pork or bacon around the leg and tie it with heavy twine at 1-inch intervals. Put meat on spit as directed for Leg and Shoulder Roasts on page 47. Insert a barbecue thermometer in heaviest part of the roast.

Arrange hot briquets to give medium heat for spit barbecuing. Attach spit to unit. Put a drip pan under meat and turn on the motor.

Barbecue veal until done, allowing about 40 minutes per pound or until thermometer registers 170°. Interior of meat should be grayish-white in color.

If desired, serve with Beets In Foil (see page 112), Barbecued Potatoes (see page 111) and one of the desserts from pages 143 to 149.

BEST-EVER LEG OF LAMB

4- to 5-pound boned leg of lamb
    (allow ⅓ pound per serving)
¼ pound bacon
¼ pound boiled ham
1 medium-size onion
½ teaspoon salt

½ teaspoon pepper
2 tablespoons red
    currant jelly
2 tablespoons coarse
    bread crumbs
Cooking oil

Early Preparation

Have meat man open the boned lamb for rolling. Then,
coarsely grind bacon, ham and onion; mix together in a
bowl with salt, pepper, jelly and bread crumbs. Lay the
boned lamb, cut-side up, on a wooden board. Spread
bacon mixture evenly over cut surface of lamb. Following the directions for Boned and Boneless Roasts on page
46, roll up lamb from the long side like a jelly roll; tie
with twine and put it on the spit rod. Brush meat with
cooking oil and insert a barbecue thermometer.

To Spit Barbecue   *Time: about 30 min. per lb.*

Arrange hot briquets to give medium heat for spit barbecuing. Attach the spit rod to the unit. Place a drip pan
under the lamb and turn on the motor. Barbecue lamb,
basting occasionally with more cooking oil. Allow about
30 minutes per pound barbecuing time for medium-done
lamb; barbecue thermometer should register 180°.

When meat is done, remove thermometer; let meat
stand about 10 minutes to firm up before carving.

LAMB SHOULDER ON THE SPIT

Buy a boned rolled shoulder roast of lamb, weighing
from 2½ to 4 pounds. Allow about ⅓ pound meat per
serving. Select and prepare one of the basting sauce
recipes from the chart on page 130. Put the rolled roast
on the spit rod as directed for Boned and Boneless Roasts

on page 46. Brush meat with some of the sauce; insert a barbecue thermometer.

Arrange hot briquets to give medium heat for spit barbecuing. Attach the spit to the unit. Place a drip pan under lamb and turn on motor. Barbecue lamb until done, brushing occasionally with more sauce. Allow 25 to 30 minutes per pound barbecuing time for medium-done lamb. Thermometer should read 180° when meat is done.

LAMB CHOPS IN THE BASKET

Select center-cut loin or rib lamb chops, cut 1 to 2 inches thick. Allow 1 to 2 chops per serving. Prepare the Curry Apricot Glaze (see below). Assemble the spit basket according to manufacturer's directions. Arrange chops in the basket and fasten the basket cover.

Arrange the hot briquets to give medium heat for spit barbecuing. Attach the spit rod with basket to the unit. Place a drip pan under the basket; start the motor. Barbecue chops, basting during the last 10 minutes of barbecuing with the glaze. For medium-rare chops 1 inch thick, barbecue about 30 minutes.

CURRY APRICOT GLAZE

1 medium-size onion, minced	½ teaspoon salt
	1 tablespoon curry powder
1 tablespoon butter or margarine	4 teaspoons vinegar
	2 tablespoons molasses
1 cup apricot puree	

Combine all ingredients in a saucepan. Cook and stir over medium heat 15 minutes. Makes 1⅓ cups.

Note: Contents of 1 jar (7¾ ounces) apricot junior fruit may be used in place of apricot puree.

STUFFED WHOLE FISH

Buy a firm-fleshed fish such as pollock or salmon, weighing about 3 pounds. Have it cleaned and the head removed. Prepare Confetti Rice Stuffing, below. Spoon stuffing into fish cavity. Close cavity and head opening by inserting small metal skewers at 1 inch intervals; lace securely with twine. Tie more twine around entire length of fish at ½ inch intervals. Put fish on spit as directed on page 48; rub with cooking oil.

Arrange hot briquets to give high heat for spit barbecuing. Attach spit to the unit. Put a drip pan under fish; start motor. Barbecue fish 15 to 20 minutes or until done, brushing fish often with more oil. Fish is done when it flakes with a fork.

CONFETTI RICE STUFFING

¾ cup cooked rice	Dash black pepper
1 clove garlic, minced	¼ cup minced green pepper
3 tablespoons minced onion	3 tablespoons minced celery
	1 peeled tomato, chopped
¾ teaspoon salt	1½ tablespoons chopped parsley

Combine all ingredients in a bowl; toss to mix well. Makes about 1½ cups stuffing.

FISH STEAKS IN A BASKET

Buy fish steaks, such as cod or halibut. Have them cut 1 inch thick. Put steaks in the spit basket (see page 51); fasten cover securely. Arrange hot briquets to give high heat for spit barbecuing. Attach spit rod with basket to unit. Put a drip pan under the basket; start motor. Barbecue steaks 12 to 18 minutes or until done, brushing them often with cooking oil.

WHOLE FISH IN SPIT BASKET

Select small whole fish such as mullet, brook trout, snappers, flounder or porgies. They should weigh no more than 2 pounds each. Have the fish cleaned and heads and tails removed. Allow 1 fish per serving.

Assemble spit basket according to manufacturer's directions. Arrange fish in the spit basket in a single layer, alternating the head and tail ends. Fasten the spit basket cover securely (see page 51). Brush fish with some cooking oil.

Arrange hot briquets to give high heat for spit barbecuing. Attach the rod with spit basket to the unit. Place a drip pan under basket; start motor.

Barbecue the fish 10 to 15 minutes, depending on thickness, or until fish flakes with a fork.

If desired, serve with one of the butters from page 118 or with one of the barbecue sauces from page 130.

LOBSTER TAILS IN A BASKET

Buy lobster tails, weighing at least ½ pound each. Allow 1 lobster tail per serving. Slit the undershell, lengthwise, with scissors; bend the tail backwards to crack the shell. Assemble the spit basket according to manufacturer's directions. Arrange lobster tails in the basket alternating tail ends. Fasten spit basket cover securely over lobster tails (see page 51). Brush the slit-side of lobster with melted butter or margarine.

Arrange hot briquets to give medium to high heat for spit barbecuing. Attach the rod with spit basket to the unit. Place a drip pan under the basket; start the motor.

Barbecue the lobster tails 20 to 25 minutes or until done. Shell is bright red when lobster is done. Brush lobster with more melted butter or margarine often during barbecuing. If desired, serve with one of the barbecue sauces from page 130 or piping hot melted butter or margarine and lemon wedges.

GLAZED CANADIAN-STYLE BACON

Buy a piece of Canadian-style bacon, weighing from 2 to 4 pounds. Allow ¼ to ⅓ pound meat per serving. Have meat man remove any casing. Prepare the Peanut Butter Glaze (see page 129). Tie twine around bacon at 1 inch intervals. Put meat on the spit as directed for Boned and Boneless Roasts on page 46; use a hammer, if necessary. Insert a barbecue thermometer in the meat.

Spit barbecue the Canadian-style bacon over medium heat allowing about 20 minutes per pound. During the last 10 to 15 minutes of barbecuing, brush the meat often with the glaze. The thermometer should read 170° when meat is done.

FILLED BOLOGNA ROLL

Buy a piece of large bologna, weighing 2 to 3 pounds. Slice bologna in half, lengthwise. With a curved grapefruit knife or the edge of a spoon, hollow out the center of each half of bologna to make a shell about 1½ inches thick. Grind the bologna taken from hollowed out portion. Mix ground meat with some drained pickle relish and a little grated Cheddar cheese.

Pack all the mixture into half of the bologna, mounding it up as necessary. Top with second half of the bologna; press firmly together. Tie twine around each end of bologna to hold halves together. Wrap several slices of salt pork or bacon around outside bologna; tie with more twine at 1½ inch intervals. Put bologna on spit as directed for Boned and Boneless Roasts on page 46, making sure one tine of each fork goes into each half bologna.

Spit barbecue the roll over medium heat until bacon is crisp and meat is heated through, or about 20 minutes. Brush meat occasionally during barbecuing with pan drippings. Slice barbecued meat and serve in buttered buns topped with your favorite barbecue sauce.

GLAZED CAPONS

6- to 8-pound ready-to-cook capons
  (allow ¾ to 1 pound meat per serving)
Salt
Cooking oil
Cranberry Glaze (see page 129)

Early Preparation

Wash capons thoroughly; pat dry with paper towels. Sprinkle the body cavity of each capon with 1 to 2 tablespoons salt. Put capons on spit as directed for Poultry on page 49. Insert barbecue thermometer. Brush capons with cooking oil. Prepare the Cranberry Glaze.

To Spit Barbecue   *Time: about 15 min. per lb.*

Arrange hot briquets to give medium heat for spit barbecuing. Attach the spit to the unit. Put a drip pan under the capons. Turn on the motor. Barbecue birds until done, allowing about 15 minutes per pound. The thermometer should register 190°. Brush birds often with the pan drippings or cooking oil during barbecuing. Then, during last 10 or 15 minutes, brush the birds often with the Cranberry Glaze.

CHICKENS FOR THE SPIT

Buy 2- to 3½-pound ready-to-cook roasting chickens. Allow ½ chicken per serving. Wash chickens thoroughly; pat dry with paper towels. Put 2 to 3 teaspoons salt in the body cavity of each chicken. Put birds on spit as directed on page 49. Insert a barbecue thermometer.

Arrange hot briquets to give medium heat for spit barbecuing. Attach the spit to the unit. Put a drip pan under the birds. Turn on the motor. Barbecue the birds until done, allowing about 20 minutes per pound. Thermometer should register 190°.

ORANGE GLAZED DUCKLING

4- to 5-pound ready-to-cook duckling
(allow about 1 pound duckling per serving)
2 quarts stuffing, rice or bread (see pages 77 to 80)
Orange Marmalade Glaze (see recipe below)

Early Preparation

Fill neck and body cavities of duckling with the prepared stuffing. Close cavities with skewers; lace with twine. Put bird on spit as directed on page 49.

To Spit Barbecue   *Time: 15 to 20 min. per lb.*

Arrange hot briquets to give medium heat for spit barbecuing. Attach spit to unit. Put a drip pan under the duckling; turn on motor. Barbecue bird until done, allowing 15 to 20 minutes per pound, basting it occasionally with drippings. During last 15 to 20 minutes of barbecuing, baste bird often with the glaze.

ORANGE MARMALADE GLAZE

2 chicken bouillon cubes	**3 tablespoons catchup**
½ cup hot water	**4 teaspoons soy sauce**
½ cup orange marmalade	**1 clove garlic, crushed**
3 tablespoons vinegar	**Dash pepper**

Put bouillon cubes into a bowl; add water and stir to dissolve cubes. Add remaining ingredients; mix well.

ROAST GOOSE

Select a goose, weighing from 10 to 12 pounds. Prepare it by the same method used for duckling, above; allow about 20 minutes per pound for barbecuing.

STUFFINGS

Stuffing can add a new flavor to food or change the existing one. It can add richness to a lean meat or counteract the richness of a fatty one, depending upon the recipe you select. Stuffing will always improve the appearance of poultry or game. And, remember, it also increases the number of servings.

The quantity of stuffing to make can only be estimated. For ready-to-cook turkeys and chickens, allow ¾ to 1 cup stuffing per pound. However, figure on only ½ to ¾ cup stuffing per pound for boned rolled meat. Most of the stuffing recipes below can be doubled or tripled or divided in half to suit your needs. Just be careful not to pack the stuffing too tightly since it swells as it heats and will become compact.

BREAD STUFFING

¼ cup butter or margarine	½ teaspoon poultry
¼ cup chopped onion	seasoning
⅓ cup chopped celery	Giblets, cooked and chopped
1 teaspoon salt	3 to 4 cups soft bread crumbs
¼ teaspoon pepper	or cubes

½ to 1 cup giblet stock or milk, if desired

Melt the butter in a small skillet. Add the onion and celery. Cook onion and celery over low heat until tender but not brown, stirring occasionally. Stir in salt, pepper and poultry seasoning. Add giblets. Put bread crumbs in a large bowl. Add giblet mixture and toss lightly. If a moist stuffing is desired, pour stock or milk over surface, stirring lightly. Stuff neck and body cavities of poultry or game lightly with stuffing. Makes about 4 cups stuffing.

Packaged bread crumbs may be used in place of soft crumbs but increase the quantity of liquid accordingly.

YAM AND SAUSAGE STUFFING

¾ pound pork sausage meat
1 medium-size onion, minced
¾ cup minced celery
2 cups fine dry bread crumbs
4 cups hot, mashed yams
¾ cup minced apples

2½ teaspoons sal
½ teaspoon pepper
½ teaspoon nutmeg
Dash ground cloves
⅛ teaspoon poultry
   seasoning

Cook meat in a skillet until brown, breaking it into small pieces as it cooks. Lift out meat. Add onion and celery to fat; cook until soft but not brown. Mix cooked meat with bread crumbs and next 7 ingredients. Mix in onion mixture. Makes about 2 quarts.

MUSHROOM STUFFING

2 cans (4 ounces each)
   sliced mushrooms
½ cup minced onion
1 cup butter, melted
3 quarts soft bread crumbs

1 cup finely diced celery
¼ cup chopped parsley
1 tablespoon poultry
   seasoning
Salt and pepper to taste

Drain mushrooms; save liquid. Cook mushrooms and onion in butter in a skillet until onion is tender. Mix bread crumbs and remaining ingredients plus mushroom liquid in a bowl. Toss lightly. Makes about 3½ quarts.

BANANA STUFFING

¼ cup minced onion
3 cups ½-inch soft
   bread cubes
½ cup butter or margarine, melted

¾ teaspoon salt
½ teaspoon poultry seasoning
1 cup diced, ripe bananas

Put all ingredients except butter in a bowl. Sprinkle butter over all; toss to mix. Makes about 1 quart.

CRANBERRY STUFFING

¼ cup butter or margarine	1 cup canned whole cranberry
¾ cup minced celery	sauce
1 quart dry bread crumbs	½ teaspoon oregano
1 can (9 ounces) crushed	¼ teaspoon nutmeg
pineapple, drained	1 teaspoon salt

Melt the butter in a skillet; add celery and cook, covered, until tender. Put celery into a bowl with bread crumbs and remaining ingredients. Toss to mix. Makes about 7 cups stuffing.

MIXED FRUIT STUFFING

2 packages (8 ounces each)	1 cup halved, seeded
ready-to-use bread stuffing	Tokay grapes
3 ripe bananas, mashed	2 oranges, sectioned
2 tart apples, diced	1 cup broken nut meats

Prepare bread stuffing as directed on package. Blend in bananas. Add apples and remaining ingredients; mix well. Makes about 3½ quarts stuffing.

CHESTNUT-RICE STUFFING

½ cup butter or margarine	1½ cups boiled chest-
1 can (4 ounces) sliced mushrooms	nuts, crumbled
¼ cup chopped ripe olives	1½ cups cooked rice
2 tablespoons chopped parsley	¼ cup milk
¼ cup chopped celery	Salt and pepper

Melt butter in a skillet. Drain mushrooms; save liquid. Add mushrooms, olives, parsley and celery to butter; cook and stir until celery is tender. Put mushroom mixture with reserved liquid and remaining ingredients in a bowl. Mix well. Makes about 1 quart.

APRICOT RICE STUFFING

½ cup butter or margarine, melted
¾ cup chopped celery
¾ cup minced onion
1 cup sliced fresh mushrooms
2½ cups brown rice

1 tablespoon salt
3 tablespoons sugar
1 teaspoon marjoram
1 package (11 ounces) dried apricots, sliced
1 quart water

Put butter, celery, onion and mushrooms in a skillet. Cook and stir until onion is lightly browned. Add rice, and remaining ingredients. Cover skillet. Bring mixture to a boil. Reduce heat; simmer 30 minutes or until rice is tender and all liquor is absorbed, stirring occasionally. Remove from heat. Cool; use at once or refrigerate. Makes 3 quarts.

ALMOND RICE STUFFING

¾ cup butter or margarine
¼ cup minced green pepper
1½ cups minced celery
3 cups cooked rice

¾ cup chopped toasted almonds
½ cup chopped ripe olives
Salt and pepper to taste

Melt butter in a skillet. Add green pepper and celery. Cook and stir until tender, but not browned. Combine the rice, almonds and olives in a large bowl; mix in celery mixture, salt and pepper. Makes 6 cups.

WILD RICE AND NUT STUFFING

1 cup pine nuts, toasted
3 cups cooked wild rice
1 tablespoon grated onion
⅛ teaspoon pepper

½ cup melted butter or margarine
½ teaspoon salt

Combine nuts with remaining ingredients in a bowl; toss together lightly to mix well. Makes about 4 cups.

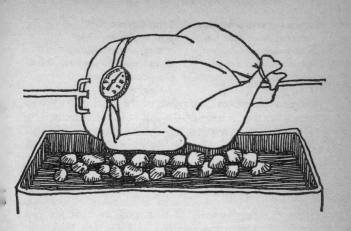

BARBECUED STUFFED TURKEY

10- to 12-pound ready-to-cook turkey
   (allow ¾ pound meat per serving)
1 recipe Apricot Rice Stuffing (see page 80)
Salt
Cooking oil

Early Preparation

Sprinkle body cavity of turkey with salt; allow about 1 teaspoon salt per pound. Fill body cavity lightly with the stuffing; lace closed, using skewers and twine. Use remaining stuffing to fill neck cavity; skewer neck skin to back. Put bird on spit (see page 49). Insert barbecue thermometer. Brush bird with cooking oil.

To Spit Barbecue   *Time: about 20 min. per lb.*

Arrange hot briquets to give medium heat for spit barbecuing. Attach spit to unit. Place a drip pan under turkey; turn on the motor. Barbecue turkey until done, allowing about 20 minutes per pound; baste with pan drippings. The thermometer should register 190°.

CHICKEN IN THE BASKET

2½-pound ready-to-cook chickens, halved
   (allow ½ chicken per serving)
Cooking oil

Early Preparation

Have meat man break the joints of the chicken halves so
they will lay flat. Assemble the spit basket as directed by
the manufacturer. Arrange the chicken halves in the spit
basket; fasten the cover securely (see page 51). Brush
chicken halves with cooking oil.

To Spit Barbecue   *Time: about 1 hour*

Arrange the hot briquets to give medium heat for spit
barbecuing. Attach the spit rod with the spit basket to
the unit. Put a drip pan under the spit basket. Turn on
the motor. Barbecue the chicken halves about 1 hour or
until done. Baste them often with cooking oil or pan
drippings during barbecuing. If desired, chicken halves
may be basted with one of the basting sauces from page
124 during barbecuing.

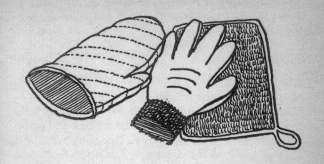

BARBECUED PHEASANT

2- to 2½-pound ready-to-cook pheasants (allow ½ pheasant per serving)
Celery leaves
Apple slices
Orange wedges
Onion slices
Bacon, sliced
Cooking oil

Early Preparation

Fill the body cavity of each pheasant with a few celery leaves, apple slices, orange wedges and onion slices. Close cavity with metal skewers; lace with twine. Place bacon slices on breast and thighs; secure with twine. Put birds on spit as directed for Poultry and Game on page 49; brush with cooking oil.

To Spit Barbecue   *Time: 15 to 20 min. per lb.*

Arrange hot briquets to give medium heat for spit barbecuing. Attach the spit to unit. Put a drip pan under pheasants; turn on the motor. Barbecue until done as desired, allowing 15 to 20 minutes per pound for a medium- or well-done pheasant; baste birds often with pan drippings. When the pheasants are done, discard seasonings in body cavities.

BARBECUED WILD DUCKS

2- to 3-pound wild ducks (allow ½ large or 1 small duck per serving)	Celery leaves
	Lemon wedges
Salt	Onion slices

Cooking Oil

Early Preparation

Wash ducks thoroughly; pat dry with paper towels. Sprinkle body cavities with a little salt. Fill each body cavity with a few celery leaves, lemon wedges and onion slices. Skewer body cavities closed; lace with twine. Put birds on spit as directed on page 49 and brush them with cooking oil. If ducks are plump, insert a barbecue thermometer.

To Spit Barbecue　　　*Time: 15 to 20 min. per lb.*

Arrange hot briquets to give medium heat for spit barbecuing. Attach spit to unit. Put a drip pan under ducks; turn on motor. Barbecue ducks until done as desired; allow 15 minutes per pound for medium-rare, 20 minutes per pound for well-done. Brush ducks often with drippings. Thermometer should read 170° or 190°.

CORNISH GAME HENS

¾- to 1-pound rock Cornish game hens
   (allow 1 hen per serving)
Salt and pepper
Cooking oil
Melted butter or margarine

Early Preparation

Sprinkle ½ teaspoon salt and a little pepper in body
cavity of each bird. Put them on spit as directed for
Poultry on page 49. Brush birds with cooking oil.

To Spit Barbecue   *Time: about 45 min.*

Arrange hot briquets to give medium heat for spit barbecuing. Attach the spit to unit and put a drip pan under
the hens. Start the motor. Barbecue hens 45 minutes to
1 hour or until done. Brush hens often with melted butter or pan drippings during barbecuing. If desired, brush
birds during the last 10 minutes of barbecuing with one
of the glazes selected from page 128. Game hens are
done when meat pulls away from the bones.

THE VERSATILE KEBOB

Long, long ago Armenian soldiers and migrating mountain folk speared pieces of wild game or lamb on their swords and roasted it over a roaring camp fire. This they called "shish kebob" meaning skewered pieces of meat.

Today, metal skewers replace the swords. And, many more foods such as fish, vegetables and even fruits are skewered to add interest to the menu. Used for appetizers, as a main course or a dessert, kebobs can make a wonderful "help yourself" affair. On a family spree or at a backyard party, grownups and small fry alike will have fun making and/or barbecuing their own.

First of all plan what type of kebobs you will serve—appetizers, a main course or a dessert. Then, get out your motorized kebober if you have one. Or, collect your individual skewers and count them to make sure you'll have plenty to go 'round. You'll need at least one per person. For appetizers, use small skewers, about 5 inches long and for desserts, slightly larger ones. But for a main course, use a jumbo-size skewer, at least

16 inches long.

There are many kinds of individual skewers to choose from. Single pointed ones, range from hand-hewn green sticks to spiral-shaped metal. But, the best kind of skewers are the two-pronged metal type. Your food will never fall off these skewers and slip into the fire!

Next, select foods which go well together. Wash and/or cut them as required. If you wish to tenderize meats or add flavor to some of the other foods, marinate them before barbecuing.

When the fire's almost ready, arrange the food on platters. Lay out the skewers, bowls of sauce for basting and, if you wish, a glaze. Now you are ready to put the food on the skewers. You can string each kind of food on a separate skewer and vary cooking times as required. Or, if you vary the size pieces you can string different foods on one skewer. If you use single pointed skewers, push the food close together to prevent it from slipping during barbecuing.

Study the tips and suggestions on pages 88 and 89 for preparing the foods. Then, everything will be ready to serve at the same time. Try some of the recipes and suggestions that follow to make any occasion a party.

Meats to Use

Select leg or shoulder of lamb, lamb or veal kidneys, sirloin tip of beef or round steak, calves liver, ready-to-eat ham, bologna, luncheon meat, precooked and link sausages, vienna sausages, frankfurters, chicken livers or hearts, Canadian bacon, raw young chicken or turkey and sliced bacon.

Fish and Sea Food to Use

Buy firm-fleshed, fresh or frozen fish or sea food, such as swordfish or salmon, oysters, scallops, or shrimp.

Fruits and Vegetables to Use

Use vegetables such as raw or cooked yams or white potatoes, zucchini squash, red and green peppers, small red or green tomatoes, small white onions, mushroom caps, eggplant, cucumber, ripe or green pitted olives. Select fruits such as raw apples, raw or canned peaches, cooked or dried apricots, dried prunes, raw bananas, raw avocados, peeled navel oranges, canned or fresh pineapple chunks and Maraschino cherries.

General Preparation

1. Cut most meats and fish into 1 to 1½ inch cubes.

2. Marinate the less tender cuts of meat and lean sea food several hours ahead of time or wrap them in sliced bacon or salt pork to barbecue.

3. To make sure all the food on one skewer will be done at the same time, select only firm fruits and vegetables. Leave very tender fruits and vegetables unpeeled. Cut soft or fast-cooking foods in large pieces and harder or slow cooking foods in smaller pieces.

4. Put the skewered foods in a hand grill to barbecue a quantity with ease.

5. Unless lean foods are wrapped in sliced bacon or salt pork, brush before and during barbecuing with cooking oil, a marinade or a sauce.

6. Barbecue kebobs over a very hot fire; turn often.

SKEWERED APPETIZERS

Appetizer kebobs make a conversation piece for any outdoor cocktail party or picnic. Here are just a few ideas intended to spur your imagination.

Fruit Tidbits

Weaving a slice of bacon between each piece of food, thread chunks of pineapple, squares of crisp red or green peppers and jumbo-size ripe olives onto skewers. Barbecue until bacon is crisp.

Pickle on a Stick

Spread thinly sliced Canadian bacon with your favorite cheese spread. Wrap meat around a small sweet pickle or a strip of dill pickle. Thread several wrapped pickles, crosswise, onto a skewer; brush with melted butter. Barbecue kebobs close to coals until heated and lightly browned. Skewer on wooden picks to serve.

Kebob Yum Yums

Wrap refrigerated pan-ready biscuits around Vienna sausages or cocktail frankfurters. Put biscuit-wrapped sausages on skewers. Then, brush with melted butter or margarine. Turn over hot coals until biscuits are golden and sausages are hot. Serve on wooden picks.

Sesame Sea Food

Prepare a marinade using equal parts of sherry wine and pineapple juice. Pour marinade over raw scallops and peeled, deveined shrimp; let stand 2 to 3 hours. Drain sea food; then brush with melted butter, margarine or cooking oil and roll in sesame seeds. Thread sea food on skewers. Barbecue over glowing coals, turning frequently. Sea food will be done as soon as outside of shrimp turns pink.

BRONCO KEBOBS

Buy round steak (cut in 1½ inch cubes), cocktail frankfurters, mushroom caps and small ripe tomatoes.

Wash the tomatoes. Wash mushrooms and peel, if necessary. Alternate round steak, frankfurters, mushroom caps and tomatoes on skewers.

Arrange the hot briquets for grill barbecuing. Brush the kebobs with cooking oil or one of the basting sauces from page 124. Lay the Bronco Kebobs on the grill close

to the hot briquets. Barbecue, turning often and basting
with more oil or sauce, 15 to 20 minutes or until the
steak is done.

FISH KEBOBS

2 pounds swordfish steaks (allow 4 ounces per serving)
Zucchini squash, about 1½ inches in diameter
Small whole ripe tomatoes
1 recipe Vermouth Basting Sauce (see page 125)

Early Preparation

Cut fish into 1-inch cubes. Cut slices of zucchini squash
¼ inch thick. Alternate fish, squash and tomatoes on
skewers.

To Grill   *Approx. Time: 8 min.*

Arrange the hot briquets for grill barbecuing. Brush
skewered foods with Vermouth Basting Sauce. Lay skewered kebobs on grill close to the coals. Barbecue, basting
with more sauce and turning often, 5 to 10 minutes or
until fish is cooked.

KIDNEY KEBOBS

Buy lamb or veal kidneys and sliced bacon. Remove
outer membrane from kidneys; cut in half, lengthwise.
Allow 6 kidneys and 6 slices of bacon per serving.

Cut bacon slices in half and wrap a piece around each
piece of kidney. String kidneys on skewers, leaving a
little space between each one. Lay kebobs on grill close
to coals. Barbecue, turning often, about 10 minutes or
just until kidneys are fork-tender. Avoid long cooking;
kidneys are done when pink cast is just disappearing
from center of meat.

ORIENTAL KEBOBS

1 pound each boned leg of lamb and top sirloin of beef
  (2 pounds of meat makes about 8 servings)
1 can (20 ounces) pineapple chunks
1 recipe Teriyaki Marinade (see below)
1 jar (9 ounces) jumbo-size pitted ripe olives, drained

Early Preparation

Cut the lamb and beef into 1½-inch cubes. Drain juice from the can of pineapple and set aside the chunks. Use juice in preparing the Teriyaki Marinade.

Marinate cubes of meat in Teriyaki Marinade for several hours at room temperature. Drain the meat and reserve the remaining marinade. Alternate meat, pineapple and olives on skewers.

To Grill   Approx. Time: 15 min.

Arrange the hot briquets for grill barbecuing. Brush skewered food with some of the reserved marinade. Lay kebobs on the grill close to the coals. Barbecue kebobs, basting with more marinade and turning frequently. Grill about 15 minutes or just until meat is done medium-rare.

TERIYAKI MARINADE

¾ cup canned pineapple   2 cloves garlic, finely
  juice   chopped
2 tablespoons soy sauce   1 small bay leaf
2 tablespoons lemon juice   ⅛ teaspoon ground cloves

Combine pineapple juice and remaining ingredients in a pint-size screw-top jar. Cover jar tightly and shake well. Use immediately or store in the refrigerator until ready to use. Makes about 1 cup.

DESSERT KEBOBS

Orange Banana Kebobs

Peel navel oranges and cut, crosswise, into ½ inch thick slices. Peel very firm bananas and cut into 1- to 1½-inch thick slices. Brush banana slices with light corn syrup and then roll in finely chopped peanuts. String alternate slices of orange and bananas on skewers.

Barbecue over hot coals just until peanuts are toasted. If desired, brush with a little creme de menthe and serve hot.

Three Fruit Kebobs

Drain canned pineapple chunks and jumbo-size Maraschino cherries; set aside. Cut unpeeled wedges of firm avocado pear. Mix together in a bowl a little orange juice, honey and a dash of cinnamon.

Alternate pineapple, cherries and avocado wedges on skewers. Brush kebobs with honey mixture. Barbecue, over hot coals just until avocado is hot, turning and brushing frequently with more honey mixture.

Kebob Mix-Up (see pic. page 88)

Mix a little lemon juice with some honey; set aside. Drain canned pineapple chunks. Cut unpeeled apples in 1½-inch wedges. Peel firm ripe bananas and cut into 2-inch lengths. Use whole tenderized apricots and dried prunes; pit prunes. Alternate fruits on skewers or on a motorized kebober see picture on page 88. Barbecue kebobs close to coals about 5 minutes, or just until apples are tender. Turn kebobs often and brush with honey mixture the last few minutes of barbecuing.

HAND GRILL SPECIALTIES

Hurray for the hand grill! This versatile little gimmick turns an open fire into a barbecue unit and a barbecue unit into a giant cooker. At the beach or picnic grounds, the hand grill can be used for everything from appetizers to desserts as well as hot dogs and hamburgers. And, used on the patio as an auxiliary grill, it can cook all those little extras which make a barbecue complete, while the main dish cooks on the unit.

Look over all the available hand grills before you purchase any. A hand grill should be made of a fairly heavy gauge, flexible metal which will hold the food firmly but still retain its shape after using. Grill handles should be long enough to prevent scorched hands during barbecuing. Some grills have wooden handles for added protection. The four basic grills are the basket with sides, flat hinged grill without sides, fine mesh grill with or without sides and the sandwich toaster.

For pieces of meat such as chicken and steak, you will need a basket grill which has sides. Thinner pieces such as chops and hamburgers are best grilled in a flat, hinged grill with grids spaced about 1 inch apart. Foods such as shrimp and chicken livers are best barbecued in a very fine mesh grill so it won't drop out.

Last, but not least important is the sandwich toaster. This hand grill is usually made of 2 hinged sides of solid cast aluminum, round or square-shaped with long handles. The sandwich is placed between the grills which shape the bread and seal the edges.

The hand grill recipes which follow are only a few of the many which can be used for barbecuing. Many of the recipes in the Grill, Spit and Kebob chapters can also be adapted to the hand grill or sandwich toaster.

STUFFED HOT DOGS

Prairie Dogs

Slit hot dogs, lengthwise, leaving one side hinged. Insert a thin strip of processed American cheese in slits and wrap each hot dog in a slice of bacon. Barbecue hot dogs in a hand grill over medium heat, turning several times, until bacon is done as desired. Serve in toasted buns with your favorite barbecue sauce.

New England's Best

Slit hot dogs, lengthwise, leaving one side hinged. Spread cut surfaces with prepared mustard; sprinkle with drained sweet pickle relish and fill with drained, canned baked beans. Secure with wooden picks. Barbecue in a hand grill over medium heat, turning several times, until beans are hot.

Dutch Dogs

Drain cooked sauerkraut. Slit hot dogs, lengthwise, leaving one side hinged; fill with drained sauerkraut. Barbecue in a hand grill over medium heat; turn several times, until sauerkraut is hot. Serve in buns.

South Sea Hot Dogs

Drain canned, crushed pineapple. Slit hot dogs, lengthwise, leaving one side hinged. Fill each hot dog with drained pineapple and wrap in a slice of bacon; secure with wooden picks. Barbecue in a hand grill over medium heat, turning several times, until bacon is done as desired. Serve in toasted frankfurter rolls.

CORNBURGERS

1 pound ground beef	⅓ cup drained canned corn
3 tablespoons pine nuts	4 teaspoons chili sauce
Salt to taste	¼ cup crumbled blue cheese

Combine the beef, pine nuts and salt in a bowl. Shape meat into 10 or 12 thin patties; set aside.

Put corn, chili sauce and blue cheese in a small bowl; mix well. Put 1 heaping tablespoon of the corn mixture in the center of each of 5 or 6 patties. Then, cover each with a second patty. Pinch the edges of the meat together to seal in the filling.

Put the patties in a hand grill and barbecue over medium heat, turning once. Allow 15 to 20 minutes for rare- to medium-done burgers. Makes 5 to 6.

JUMBO BURGER

For each Jumbo Burger, buy ½ *pound ground round steak*. Combine the beef with ½ *teaspoon salt, a dash pepper* and ½ *teaspoon minced onion* in a small bowl. Shape meat into 2 large, thin patties. Mound ¼ *cup of your favorite stuffing mixture* in the center of one patty. Top with second patty; pinch edges of meat together to seal in mixture. Put the burger in a hand grill and barbecue over medium heat, turning once.

A Jumbo Burger barbecued 3 inches from the hot briquets will take about 15 minutes.

CONEY ISLAND BURGERS

Season ground beef to taste with salt and pepper; mix in a little minced onion and chili sauce. Shape meat into an even number of thin patties. Top half the patties with a slice of processed American cheese; cover each with a second patty. Pinch edges of meat together to seal in cheese. Wrap a slice of bacon around edge of each burger; skewer with a wooden pick. Cook burgers in a hand grill over medium heat, about 15 minutes or until meat is done; turn once.

STEAK ROLLS

1 flank steak, weighing 1½ to 2 pounds	¼ cup chopped apple
	¼ cup minced onion
Teriyaki Marinade (see page 92)	1 tablespoon butter or margarine, melted
⅓ cup fine dry bread crumbs	

Score both sides of steak lightly, in crisscross fashion. Marinate steak 1 to 2 hours in Teriyaki Marinade; drain well. Save marinade for basting. Combine bread crumbs, apple, onion and butter; toss to mix well. Spread mixture over flank steak. Starting with long side, roll steak up like a jelly roll. Insert wooden picks at about 1-inch intervals. Cut flank steak between picks into 1- to 1½-inch thick diagonal slices.

Place rolls in a hand grill. Barbecue steak over medium heat, turning often and basting with reserved marinade, until done as desired. Allow about 15 minutes for medium-done steak.

PORK CHOPS SUPREME

Buy rib, center-cut, loin or shoulder pork chops, cut about 1 inch thick. Allow 1 or 2 chops per serving. Trim off excess fat. Spread both sides of chops with anchovy paste; then, dip in fine dry bread crumbs. Place chops in a hand grill; brush with cooking oil.

Barbecue chops over low heat, turning frequently and brushing with more cooking oil, until well done or, about 45 minutes.

GINGER HAM STEAK

Buy a "ready-to-eat" ham slice cut 1½ to 2 inches thick. Allow about ⅓ pound per serving. Slash fat edge of steak to prevent curling. Drain canned pineapple slices. Prepare the Ginger Glaze recipe on page 129.

Lay steak in a hand grill; arrange pineapple on top. Close grill securely. Brush both sides of steak with cooking oil and barbecue over medium heat, about 8 minutes per side; turn just once. Brush steak with Ginger Glaze during the last 5 minutes of barbecuing.

HAM ROLL UPS

For each serving, marinate *1 or 2 canned drained asparagus tips* in *French dressing* for about 1 hour. Place drained asparagus tips on *a slice of boiled ham* with *½ slice of processed American cheese;* roll ham up like a jelly roll. Wrap *a slice of bacon* around ham and secure with wooden picks; put in a hand grill and close grill securely.

Barbecue ham rolls over medium heat, turning frequently, until bacon is cooked and cheese melts.

Ham rolls barbecued 3 inches above the hot briquets take about 10 to 15 minutes.

GRILLED WAFFLES

Frozen waffles are delicious for a breakfast out-of-doors or for a sandwich in place of bread.

Place frozen waffles in a hand grill and close grill. Hold hand grill over medium heat, about 3 inches above coals. Barbecue waffles, turning once, until heated and lightly browned, about 10 minutes. Serve with butter, syrup and grilled sausages or make a sandwich using one of the fillings from page 100, if desired.

STUFFED FISH FILLETS

1 pound fish fillets, sole,
  flounder or halibut
½ cup moist bread
  crumbs
2 tablespoons butter or
  margarine, melted
½ cup grated carrot
1 tablespoon chopped
  green pepper
½ teaspoon salt
Dash black pepper
Cooking oil

If fish is frozen, thaw completely before barbecuing.
Wash fillets and pat dry with paper towels.

Combine bread crumbs and next 5 ingredients in a
small bowl. Toss stuffing mixture to mix well. Spread
1 or 2 tablespoons of the bread crumb mixture over each
fillet. Roll up fish fillets like a jelly roll; secure with
wooden picks.

Rub the hand grill with cooking oil. Put fillets in the
grill and close the grill securely. Brush fillets with cooking oil and barbecue over medium heat until done, turning frequently and brushing with more oil as required.

Fish fillets held 3 inches above the hot briquets will take
about 20 minutes. Makes about 4 servings.

CHEESE STUFFED DATES

Stuff pitted dates with thin strips of processed Cheddar
cheese. Place the cheese stuffed dates in a fine mesh hand
grill and close the grill securely.

Hold the hand grill close to the hot briquets for just 2
or 3 minutes or until the cheese melts. Better have plenty
of these dates prepared, they'll go fast.

HOT SANDWICHES

As much fun to make as they are to eat, toasted or grilled sandwiches rate high any time you barbecue them over glowing coals. Follow the general directions below, for toasted sandwiches if you prefer just to brown and heat the bread. But, for a really piping hot filling, try grilling them.

Toasted Sandwiches For each sandwich, spread 2 slices of bread with butter. Then, spread unbuttered side of 1 slice with one of the sandwich fillings selected from below; top with second slice of bread, buttered-side up. Put sandwich in grill and close grill securely. Hold grill over medium heat, turning often, until bread is golden brown and filling is warm.

Sandwiches barbecued 3 inches from the hot briquets will take about 8 minutes.

Grilled Sandwiches First spread one side of 1 slice of bread with a sandwich filling selected from below; top with a second slice of bread. Then, brush the outsides of bread with melted butter or margarine.

Place the sandwich between 2 sheets of aluminum foil in a hand grill and barbecue over medium heat, turning often, until filling is very hot or melted, about 10 minutes. And for a special treat, place sandwiches in a cast aluminum sandwich toaster. This type hand grill seals in and cooks the filling.

Grilled Cheese

Place a slice of American cheese between 2 slices of your favorite bread; follow general directions, above, for Grilled Sandwiches. If you have small pieces of sharp Cheddar cheese leftover, put through the food chopper together with some green pepper and onion. Spread on bread and grill, following general directions for Grilled Sandwiches, above.

Virginia's Favorite

Combine *½ cup homogenized peanut butter, ¼ cup crumbled crisp bacon* and *¼ cup sweet pickle relish*. Spread peanut butter mixture between slices of bread and toast or grill as directed above. Makes enough filling for 3 sandwiches.

Chicken Special

Mix together *1⅓ cups minced, cooked chicken, ⅓ cup minced celery, ⅓ cup finely chopped walnuts* and *¼ cup mayonnaise*. Season to taste with *salt and pepper*. Spread mixture between slices of bread and toast or grill as directed, above. Fills 6 sandwiches.

Deep Sea Dive

Use *1½ cups cooked fish or sea food* such as flaked tuna or crabmeat. Mix fish with *½ cup chopped celery, ¼ cup chopped stuffed olives* and *2 tablespoons lemon juice*. Moisten with enough *canned condensed tomato soup* so mixture spreads easily. Spread fish mixture between slices of bread and toast or grill as directed, above. Makes enough for 8 sandwiches.

Peach Sandwich Pie

For each pie, spread *2 slices of white bread* with *some butter or margarine*. Place 1 slice of the bread in a cast aluminum sandwich toaster, buttered-side down. Peel and slice *1 peach* and put into a bowl with *3 chopped pitted dates* and *1 tablespoon sugar;* toss to mix well. Spoon mixture onto bread. Sprinkle with *a little cinnamon* and dot with *a little butter or margarine*. Top with a second slice of bread, buttered-side up. Close the grill securely over the sandwich.

  Place the hand grill over low heat and barbecue pies, turning frequently, 15 to 20 minutes or, until bread is golden brown and peaches are cooked. Sprinkle pies with *a little confectioners' sugar* and serve warm.

HOT POT TALK

The basic list of barbecue cookware is the heavy skillet, griddle, Dutch oven and, of course, the coffee pot! Pans should be made of heavy cast iron or aluminum, preferably with long handles. Heavy metals take a lot of hard wear and hold the heat best.

So, be it breakfast at sunrise or dinner at sunset, do get out in the open and rattle those pots and pans! The recipes in this section are dedicated to the camper who prefers a simple one-dish meal cooked over a camp stove, as well as to the patio chef, with the deluxe barbecued meal in mind.

MEXICAN BUN SANDWICH

½ pound bacon, diced
1 cup (4 ounces) dried
   beef, shredded
¾ cup chili sauce

1 cup diced processed
   Cheddar cheese
⅓ cup pickle relish
8 to 10 hamburger buns

8 to 10 slices onion, ¼-inch thick

Put the bacon in a skillet; cook over medium heat until crisp. Discard all but about ¼ cup of the fat. Add the beef and next 3 ingredients; continue to cook, stirring constantly until cheese melts.

Split hamburger buns and toast. Spoon mixture on half the buns; top each with an onion slice. Then, cover with remaining buns. Makes 8 to 10 servings.

BUN BURGERS

Butter or margarine
1 pound ground round steak
1 cup chopped onion
1 cup chopped celery
1 cup chopped green pepper
1 teaspoon salt
⅛ teaspoon black pepper
1 can (10½ ounces) condensed tomato soup
1 to 2 teaspoons barbecue sauce
Hamburger buns, slit

Melt 1 tablespoon of the butter in a heavy skillet over high heat. Put meat in skillet. Brown it, stirring occasionally and breaking it up into pieces with the side of a spoon as it cooks. Add onions, celery, green pepper, salt, black pepper, soup and barbecue sauce. Continue to cook over low heat, stirring occasionally, 20 to 25 minutes or until vegetables are tender.

Meanwhile, spread hamburger buns with softened butter. When mixture is heated, spoon into the buns. Makes 8 to 10 servings.

'ORLEANS BURGER

1 tablespoon fat or cooking oil
1 pound ground round steak
⅓ cup chopped onion
1 can (10½ ounces) condensed chicken gumbo soup
2 tablespoons chili sauce
2 tablespoons prepared mustard
¼ teaspoon pepper
½ teaspoon salt
8 hamburger buns, slit
Butter or margarine, softened

Melt fat in a heavy skillet. Put meat and onion into the skillet. Brown meat, stirring occasionally and breaking it up into small pieces, with the side of a spoon, as it cooks. Stir in soup, chili sauce, mustard, pepper and salt. Simmer mixture, covered, over low heat about 5 minutes or until thoroughly heated; stir occasionally. Spread hamburger buns with butter. Spoon mixture into the buns.

HAWAIIAN PORK

1 pound boned pork shoulder, sliced ¼ inch thick	1½ teaspoons salt
	¼ teaspoon black pepper
Butter or margarine	2 tablespoons cornstarch
1 medium-size onion, minced	2 tablespoons brown sugar
1 green pepper, cut in strips	2 tablespoons lemon juice
1 cup water	1 tablespoon soy sauce
¼ teaspoon mace	1 can (20 ounces) crushed
⅛ teaspoon ginger	pineapple

Hamburger buns, slit

Have pork tenderized; cut into 1-inch squares.

Melt 1 tablespoon of the butter in a skillet. Add meat and onion; stir to brown well. Stir in green pepper and next 5 ingredients. Bring mixture to a boil; reduce heat to low. Simmer, covered, 30 to 35 minutes or until meat is tender.

Meanwhile, combine cornstarch and next 3 ingredients. Stir in pineapple; mix well. Pour pineapple over meat; cook and stir until sauce thickens. Spread buns with butter. Spoon mixture onto the buns. Makes 8 to 10 servings.

WESTERN BURGERS

Butter or margarine, softened	2 teaspoons chopped stuffed olives
Hamburger buns, sliced	
1 pound pork sausage meat	2 eggs, slightly beaten
½ cup chopped green pepper	½ cup fine dry bread crumbs
¼ cup chopped onion	

¼ cup water

Spread butter on hamburger buns; set aside. Combine all ingredients in a bowl; stir to mix well. Shape meat mixture into 6 large or 8 small patties. Fry patties over low heat, turning often, 15 to 20 minutes or until done. Meat is grayish-white in color when done. Makes 6 to 8 servings.

PEPPER STEAK

1 pound round steak	4 green peppers, cut in
¼ cup cooking oil	1-inch pieces
1 teaspoon salt	1 cup sliced celery
Dash pepper	1 cup beef bouillon
¼ cup sliced green onions or	2 tablespoons cornstarch
finely diced onion	¼ cup water
1 clove garlic	2 teaspoons soy sauce

Hot cooked rice

Cut steak diagonally into thin slices, then into 2-inch pieces. Heat oil with salt and pepper in a skillet. Add meat, cook over high heat until brown, stirring frequently. Add next 5 ingredients. Cover and cook over medium heat until vegetables are crisply tender, about 10 minutes. Combine cornstarch, water and soy sauce. Add to meat; cook and stir until mixture is thickened, about 5 minutes. Serve on hot, cooked rice. Makes 4 servings.

CURRIED RICE

1 cup rice	3 tablespoons minced parsley
3 tablespoons butter or	3 bouillon cubes
margarine	2½ cups boiling water
⅓ cup chopped onion	1½ teaspoon curry powder

Pinch thyme

Wash rice and drain well. Melt the butter in a heavy skillet. Add rice and cook over medium heat, stirring frequently, 10 to 15 minutes or until rice turns a light brown. Add onion and parsley; continue to cook and stir until onion is soft.

Dissolve bouillon cubes in the water. Add bouillon, curry and thyme to the rice and stir to mix well. Cook, covered, over low heat, about 20 minutes or until rice is tender and liquid is absorbed. Stir occasionally to prevent sticking. Makes 4 to 6 servings.

LET'S HAVE A HOBO PICNIC!

Plan a hobo-style picnic for the least muss and fuss for everyone concerned. You'll need lots of clean 1-pound size coffee cans, so start collecting them 'way ahead of time. Prepare all the food at home and then put enough food for one person in a can or use one can for several servings of each of the foods. In either case, be sure to label the cans! Keep perishable foods cool until they reach the barbecue fire. Take plenty of paper plates, knives, forks and spoons and watch the "hobos" dig in.

HOBO STEAK FOR ONE

¼ pound round steak, cut ¾ inch thick
Fat or cooking oil
2 slices potato, cut ½ inch thick
¼ cup water
2 tablespoons canned sliced mushrooms, drained
¼ cup onion rings

1 small tomato, quartered
1 tablespoon sliced pitted olives
1½ teaspoons butter or margarine
1 teaspoon salt
Few grains pepper
⅛ teaspoon Worcestershire sauce

⅛ teaspoon garlic salt

For each hobo dinner you will need a pound-size coffee can with a cover. Have meat man tenderize steak. Heat a little fat in a heavy skillet. Brown steak on both sides and remove from heat.

Put potato slices in bottom of coffee can. Lay meat on top of the potatoes. Add water, mushrooms, onion rings, tomato, olives and butter. Sprinkle with salt, pepper, Worcestershire sauce and garlic salt. Cover can tightly.

Arrange hot briquets for grill barbecuing or use a bed of hot ashes. Nestle can among coals but do not set can directly on top of them. Barbecue about 50 minutes or until vegetables are tender.

HOBO SPECIAL FOR ONE

½ pound ground beef	2 small onions, peeled
¼ teaspoon salt	3 slices potato, cut
Dash pepper	½ inch thick
1 tablespoon chopped parsley	10 ripe olives
1 teaspoon chopped onion	½ ear of corn
1 small carrot, cut in strips	Salt and pepper to taste

For each hobo dinner you will need a pound-size coffee can with cover.

Combine beef, salt, pepper, parsley and onion in a bowl. Shape meat mixture into a large patty the size of the bottom of the coffee can; lay patty in the bottom of the can. First put carrot strips, then onions, potato slices, olives and finally corn on top of beef in can; sprinkle with salt and pepper. Cover can tightly.

Arrange hot briquets for grill barbecuing or use a bed of hot ashes. Nestle can among hot coals but do not set can directly on top of them. Barbecue about 1 hour or until vegetables are tender.

HOBO ORANGE RICE

1 cup water	1 package (5 ounces) pre-
½ cup thawed frozen orange	cooked rice
juice concentrate	1 tablespoon butter
1¼ teaspoon salt	¼ teaspoon nutmeg
	Dash pepper

For each recipe you will need a pound-size coffee can and cover. Combine the water, orange juice and salt in the can.

Arrange hot briquets for grill barbecuing. Put can on grill, close to coals and heat contents to boiling. Remove can from heat; add and stir in rice, butter, nutmeg and pepper. Cover can tightly; set along side of grill, away from heat. Let can stand, covered, 12 to 14 minutes or until rice is tender. Makes 3 cups.

FRUITS—VEGETABLES—BREADS

Fruits, vegetables and hot breads, served as appetizers or main course accompaniments, are always a welcome addition to any barbecue. Cook them on top of a grill, in a hand grill or, on skewers. Or, wrap them in aluminum foil and nestle them among glowing coals.

Barbecuing on the grill or in foil is best for foods requiring long, slow cooking. Skewer and hand grill cooking is best for foods that require very little cooking, or just heating. But, try the recipes that follow and see for yourself. Additional recipes using fruits and vegetables may be found on pages 86 to 93.

SHERRIED PINEAPPLE BOAT

Buy a medium-size ripe whole pineapple. Allow 1 pineapple for 4 people. Cut pineapple in half, lengthwise, to make it boat shaped. But, be sure you have some leaves left on each half.

Prepare each pineapple half as follows: First, cut around the outer edges of the pineapple, with a grapefruit knife, being careful not to penetrate the peel. Then, loosen the core by cutting down, lengthwise, along the sides of it; a small paring knife is best to use. Next, make bite-size sections of fruit by slicing it crosswise, on each side of the core; leave the sections and core in place.

Sprinkle cut surfaces of pineapple generously with sugar and top with a little orange juice. Place each pineapple half, cut-side up, on a single thickness of aluminum foil. Wrap foil tightly around pineapple; let stand 30 minutes.

Nestle the foil-wrapped pineapple, cut-side up, among the coals, not directly on top. Heat pineapple, without turning, just until warm or 20 to 30 minutes. Unwrap pineapple immediately and sprinkle with a little sherry wine, or creme de menthe. If desired, lay sprigs of mint or Maraschino cherries on pineapple core to garnish it. Serve with wooden picks.

APPLE ON A STICK

Select a medium-size eating apple; wash and put on a skewer. Roast or hold apple directly over coals until fork-tender or 20 to 30 minutes; turn often. Peel off skin and dip apple in melted butter; sprinkle with cinnamon and roll in brown sugar. Return sugar-coated apple to heat, rotating it slowly for 10 minutes or until sugar carmelizes. Cool and serve on the skewer.

PEACHES 'N' BERRIES

For each serving, select a large, firm, ripe free-stone peach; cut in half, remove pit and peel. Lay peach halves, cut-side up, on a double thickness of aluminum foil. Pile fresh, ripe blueberries in center of each half. Sprinkle peach with a little brown sugar and a few drops lemon juice; wrap in foil.

Nestle foil-wrapped peach, cut-side up, among coals, not directly on top. Barbecue the peach, without turning, just until fork-tender or about 15 minutes. Or, grill barbecue about 25 minutes over medium heat. Unwrap, serve warm.

WINE FLAVORED GRAPEFRUIT

For each 2 servings, cut a grapefruit in half, crosswise. Remove the seeds. Cut out the core and loosen each section from the membrane with a sharp, pointed knife. In the center of each half, pour a little muscatel wine. Then, top with a little honey and sprinkle with nutmeg. Wrap each grapefruit half securely in a double thickness of heavy-duty aluminum foil.

Lay grapefruit, cut-side up, directly on top of coals or on grill. Barbecue fruit, leaving cut-side up, about 10 minutes on coals or about 20 minutes on grill over medium heat. Unwrap grapefruit; serve warm.

MINTED PEARS

For each serving, drain 2 canned pear halves. Lay pears, cut-side up, on a double thickness of heavy-duty aluminum foil. Put several pieces of coarsely chopped, crystallized ginger and a little applemint jelly in center of each half. Wrap pears, cut-side up, in foil.

Lay foil-wrapped pears, cut-side up, directly on the hot briquets or on the grill. Barbecue pears, without turning, about 5 minutes on briquets or, about 12 minutes on the grill over medium heat. Unwrap pears and serve immediately.

BARBECUED POTATOES

Use medium-size white potatoes, sweets or yams. Scrub well; dry. Rub skins with soft butter or margarine. Wrap each potato in a double thickness of aluminum foil.

Lay potatoes on coals. Barbecue medium-size white potatoes, turning occasionally, 45 to 60 minutes; sweets or yams 30 to 45 minutes. Potatoes are done if they feel soft when gently pressed with an asbestos-gloved thumb.

When soft, slit foil, cut potato in both directions; press gently to break open. Fluff with a fork; season with butter, salt and pepper.

HERB SEASONED CARROTS

For each serving, select several small, tender carrots. Scrape carrots, if desired, then rub with butter or margarine. Place carrots on a double thickness of heavy-duty aluminum foil. Sprinkle with a little thyme, salt and several tablespoons water; wrap in foil.

Lay wrapped carrots on coals; barbecue, turning occasionally, about 1 hour or until fork-tender.

APPLE STUFFED ACORN SQUASH

Cut *one medium-size acorn squash* in half, lengthwise; scoop out seeds. Put *1 cup chopped apple* and *2 tablespoons brown sugar* in a bowl; toss to mix. Fill center of squash with apple mixture. Dot with *butter or margarine;* sprinkle with *cinnamon* and *a little salt.* Wrap squash in heavy-duty aluminum foil.

Place foil-wrapped squash, cut-side up, directly on the coals. Barbecue squash, leaving cut-side up, 40 to 50 minutes or until fork-tender. Serves 3 to 4.

SURPRISE PACKS

Slice zucchini squash, crosswise, in ¼-inch slices. Place individual portions on double thicknesses of aluminum foil. Add cubed fresh tomato, thinly sliced celery, salt, pepper, a pinch of oregano and a pat of butter or margarine; wrap in foil. Barbecue vegetables directly on briquets 14 to 16 minutes or on grill, close to coals, about 25 minutes; turn once.

BEETS IN FOIL

For each serving, select several small, tender beets. Trim off stem ends and wash beets thoroughly. Place on a double thickness of heavy-duty aluminum foil. Sprinkle them with a little salt; add a little water and dot with butter or margarine. Wrap in foil.

Place foil-wrapped beets directly on coals. Barbecue, turning occasionally, about 1 hour or until fork-tender. When done, open foil and slip skin off beets. Serve immediately or rewrap in foil to keep hot.

GREEN BEANS SOUTHERN-STYLE

Drain contents of *1 can (15½ ounces) whole or cut green beans.* Add *½ cup chopped pecans,* or *¼ cup canned, sliced mushrooms, salt and pepper to taste;* toss to mix well. Divide into individual portions and lay each on a double thickness of heavy-duty aluminum foil. Top each portion with *a little butter or margarine* and wrap tightly in the foil.

Heat foil-wrapped green beans on the grill about 20 minutes, turning once. Or, heat directly on top of the hot briquets 8 to 10 minutes, turning often. Makes 4 to 5 servings.

Thawed, frozen cut beans may also be barbecued on the briquets. Heat about 10 minutes; turn often.

BARBECUED CORN

Corn in Wet Newspaper

Select fresh sweet young corn. Allow 1 to 2 ears per serving. Strip husks down to end of corn. Do not tear off. Remove silk. Let corn stand in salted ice water 20 minutes to 1 hour; then drain well. Brush with softened

butter or margarine and sprinkle with salt and pepper. Bring husks up around corn; be sure all kernels are covered. For each ear of corn, immerse 4 thicknesses of newspaper in water, soaking it completely. Wrap each ear in wet newspaper.

Arrange hot briquets for grill barbecuing, or use a bed of hot ashes. Nestle the newspaper-wrapped corn among the coals. Barbecue, turning frequently, about 25 minutes. As newspaper dries out, sprinkle it with more water to prevent burning during barbecuing. Unwrap corn and serve immediately.

Corn in Foil

Select fresh sweet young corn. Allow 1 to 2 ears per serving. Strip husks down to end of corn; do not tear off. Remove silk. Brush kernels with softened butter or margarine and sprinkle with salt and pepper. Bring husks up around corn. Be sure all kernels are covered. Wrap each ear in a double thickness of heavy-duty aluminum foil; twist ends well.

Arrange hot briquets for grill barbecuing and barbecue corn in foil as directed above for Corn in Wet Newspaper. No sprinkling is required.

SEA ISLAND ORANGES

For each serving, peel *1 seedless orange;* separate into sections. Put orange on a double thickness of heavy-duty aluminum foil. Sprinkle fruit generously with *brown sugar.* Add *a dash of cinnamon, 1 tablespoon of light rum* and *1 teaspoon of butter or margarine.* Wrap securely in foil. Barbecue on grill over medium heat 12 to 15 minutes or, on briquets 8 to 12 minutes.

BAR-B-QUED BANANAS

Use firm ripe bananas; allow 1 or 2 per serving. Peel bananas; put on a double thickness of heavy-duty aluminum foil and brush with lemon juice. Sprinkle fruit with brown sugar; dot with butter and wrap in the foil.

Lay foil-wrapped bananas directly on hot briquets and barbecue 7 to 9 minutes; turn often. Or, grill barbecue, laying the foil-wrapped fruit on the grill over medium heat. Barbecue 14 to 17 minutes; turn often. To serve, open aluminum foil and garnish bananas with red currant jelly and a little shredded coconut.

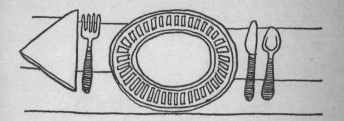

WISCONSIN FRENCH BREAD

Cut a long loaf of French bread in half, lengthwise. Brush cut-side of bread generously with Garlic Butter (see recipe on page 118); sprinkle with grated Parmesan or sharp Cheddar cheese. Put the halves of bread together and wrap securely in a single thickness of heavy-duty aluminum foil. Barbecue on grill, close to coals, until cheese melts and bread is heated, or about 15 minutes; turn occasionally.

POPPY SEED LOAF

Cut a small loaf of unsliced white bread in half, lengthwise, leaving bottom hinged. Then, cut bread, crosswise, into eighths. Place it on a single thickness of aluminum foil. Brush all surfaces with melted butter or one of the butters from page 118. Sprinkle top, sides and cut surfaces with poppy seeds. Wrap bread securely in the foil. Barbecue on grill, close to coals, until heated or about 15 minutes.

SLIM STICKS

Put packaged bread sticks on a double thickness of heavy-duty aluminum foil. Brush sticks with melted butter or margarine seasoned to taste with a few drops Tabasco sauce, a dash paprika and minced garlic. Wrap securely in the foil.

Barbecue bread sticks on grill, close to coals about 5 minutes or, until thoroughly heated; turn often.

OLIVE AND CHEESE BREAD

Cut a long loaf of French bread diagonally, in 1½-inch slices, leaving one side hinged. Spread Mustard Butter (see recipe on page 118) in diagonal cuts. Then, insert a half slice of processed American cheese and a few slices of ripe olives in each cut. Wrap bread in a single thickness of heavy-duty aluminum foil.

Arrange hot briquets for grill barbecuing. Put bread on grill, close to coals. Barbecue, turning often, until cheese melts or about 20 minutes.

FIRESIDE BISCUITS

Use refrigerated pan-ready biscuits or packaged biscuit mix. If packaged biscuit mix is used, prepare as directed and cut into ¼-inch thick squares.

Place a large heavy skillet over low heat either directly on the coals or on the grill. Put several tablespoons butter or margarine in the hot skillet. Add a little crushed garlic or a pinch of your favorite herb to the butter, if desired. Arrange biscuits in butter and cover skillet tightly with a cover or a piece of aluminum foil. Cook biscuits 4 to 6 minutes or until golden brown on bottom. Turn biscuits and continue to cook, covered, 6 to 8 minutes longer or until second side is golden brown. Uncover; stand biscuits on sides and continue to cook and turn until evenly browned. Serve biscuits at once.

DEVILED HAM BUNS

Combine canned deviled ham spread, a little mayonnaise, a few drops Worcestershire sauce, a dash pepper and some chopped parsley. Spread mixture on split hamburger or frankfurter buns; put together. Wrap securely in a single thickness of aluminum foil. Lay foil-wrapped buns on grill close to coals and barbecue until heated or about 10 minutes; turn once.

BLUE CHEESE TEASERS

Use ready-to-serve package fan tan rolls. Remove them from the package and place on a single thickness of heavy-duty aluminum foil. Brush generously with Blue Cheese Butter (see page 118) and wrap securely in foil. Lay foil-wrapped rolls on grill, close to coals and barbecue until thoroughly heated, or about 15 minutes; turn frequently.

PATIO PICK UPS

1 small loaf of Italian bread	1 tablespoon chopped
¼ cup butter or margarine, softened	pimiento
	3 tablespoons chopped
1 tablespoon prepared mustard	parsley
½ cup minced mild onion	2 tablespoons sesame seeds

Cut loaf of bread in half, lengthwise. Combine butter, mustard, onion, pimiento and parsley. Divide butter mixture between the two halves of bread and spread over the surface. Sprinkle sesame seeds on top of butter mixture. Wrap each half of bread in a single thickness of aluminum foil. Place foil-wrapped bread on grill, close to coals; barbecue until heated or about 15 minutes, turning once. To serve, open foil and cut bread, crosswise, at 1 inch intervals.

SAVORY BUTTERS

Mustard Butter

Soften *½ cup butter or margarine* in a small bowl. Add and stir in *2 teaspoons prepared mustard* and *a few drops Worcestershire sauce.*

Garlic Butter

Soften *½ cup butter or margarine* in a bowl. Crush a *peeled clove of garlic;* add and stir into butter.

Blue Cheese Butter

Soften *½ cup butter or margarine* in a bowl. Add and stir in *2 to 3 tablespoons crumbled blue cheese.*

Lemon Butter

Melt *½ cup butter or margarine* in a saucepan. Stir in *2 tablespoons lemon juice, ¾ teaspoon salt, a dash pepper* and *2 tablespoons minced parsley.*

FLAVOR HELPS FOR MEATS

Herbed or spice-flavored sauces and marinades go hand in hand with expert barbecuing and are so easy to prepare. The only secret is understanding how best to use each kind. So, read the recommendations below, glance over the suggestion charts that follow and, then let yourself go!

Marinades are used before barbecuing to give flavor to meats and sometimes to tenderize. To tenderize they must contain some lemon juice, vinegar or wine. Some less tender cuts of meat must be marinated overnight, but most need only to be marinated a few hours at room temperature. Some marinades react with aluminum, so always put them in glass or enamel containers. When refrigerating a marinade, cover the container tightly to prevent odors from penetrating other foods. Most marinades can also be used as basting sauces.

Basting Sauces are used to keep meats moist during cooking and impart a subtle flavor. For long-cooking periods, use sauces containing oil. Those containing tomato should be applied just the last 10 minutes of barbecuing, but others may be applied from the start.

Glazes are used to give meats that frosted, shiny, centerpiece look and a subtle flavoring. A glaze generally contains sugar in some form such as honey, syrup, jelly or a preserve. So, to prevent a glaze from burning, brush it on the meat only during the last 5 to 15 minutes of barbecuing.

Barbecue Sauces served with any meat, poultry or fish give added zest and are extremely versatile. Most barbecue sauces make delicious dunks for appetizers as well as main dish accompaniments. And sauces, slightly thin in consistency, can be used for basting.

Marinade Selection Chart

Beef Good With
California Marinade, p. 123
Teriyaki Marinade, p. 92
Rum Marinade, p. 32
Tarragon Marinade, p. 121

Veal Good With
Hawaiian Marinade, p. 123
Mint Marinade, p. 31
Herb Marinade, p. 39
Tarragon Marinade, p. 121

Ham or Pork Good With
Hawaiian Marinade, p. 123
California Marinade, p. 123
Oriental Spice Mixture, p. 62
Rum Marinade, p. 32
Honey-Spice Marinade, p. 121
Sharp-Spicy Marinade, p. 122

Lamb Good With
Mint Marinade, p. 31

Sharp-Spicy Marinade, p. 122
Teriyaki Marinade, p. 92
Speedy Marinade, p. 121

Poultry Good With
Honey-Spice Marinade, p. 121
Speedy Marinade, p. 121
Wine Marinade, p. 123
Tarragon Marinade, p. 121
Oriental Spice Mixture, p. 62

Fish and Sea Food Good With
Sauterne Marinade, p. 122
Herb Marinade, p. 39
Sportsman's Marinade, p. 122
Soy Marinade, p. 120
Game Marinade, p. 42

Game Good With
Sauterne Marinade, p. 122
Sportsman's Marinade, p. 122
Game Marinade, p. 42

SOY MARINADE

Put *½ cup soy sauce, 1 clove garlic, crushed* and *½ cup cooking oil* in a screw-top jar and cover. Shake marinade well before using. Makes about 1 cup.

SPEEDY MARINADE

½ teaspoon rosemary	½ teaspoon thyme
½ teaspoon tarragon	½ cup cooking oil
1 cup lemon juice	

Put all ingredients except lemon juice in a small saucepan; heat. Add lemon juice; stir to mix well. Cool and pour over meat to marinate. Or store marinade, covered, in refrigerator until ready to use. Makes 1½ cups.

HONEY-SPICE MARINADE

2 teaspoons ginger	¼ cup honey
2 teaspoons dry mustard	½ cup cooking oil
2 teaspoons salt	½ cup lemon juice
¼ teaspoon pepper	2 to 3 cloves garlic, peeled
2 tablespoons soy sauce	and crushed

Combine all ingredients in a pint-size, screw-top jar. Cover and shake to mix well. Store, covered, in refrigerator until ready to use. Makes about 1½ cups.

TARRAGON MARINADE

1 large onion	¼ teaspoon dry mustard
1 cup cooking oil	1 teaspoon salt
¼ cup tarragon vinegar	3 cloves garlic, minced
½ cup burgundy wine	1 whole bay leaf
¼ cup lemon juice	6 peppercorns

Peel and slice onion, ¼ inch thick. Separate onion into rings; put into a large, screw-top jar. Add remaining ingredients; cover and shake vigorously. Chill until ready to use. Shake well just before using. If desired, serve onion slices raw or, cooked with a little butter in foil on coals. Makes about 2¼ cups.

SHARP-SPICY MARINADE

½ cup water   2 tablespoons minced onion
½ cup wine vinegar   2 bay leaves
½ cup cooking oil   4 whole cloves

Combine water, vinegar and oil in a pint-size, screw-top jar. Add remaining ingredients. Cover jar and shake vigorously. Refrigerate marinade, covered, until ready to use. Makes about 1½ cups marinade.

SAUTERNE MARINADE

⅓ cup sauterne wine   1 small bay leaf
⅓ cup cooking oil   1 teaspoon paprika
2 tablespoons lime or   1 tablespoon crushed juniper
  lemon juice   berries, if desired

Combine all ingredients in a pint-size, screw-top jar. Cover jar and shake vigorously. Store in refrigerator until ready to use. Makes about ¾ cup marinade.

SPORTSMAN'S MARINADE

1½ cups vinegar   1 medium-size onion, finely
1 cup Burgundy wine   chopped
¼ cup cooking oil   2 tablespoons chopped celery
1 bay leaf   2 tablespoons chopped parsley
¼ teaspoon thyme   ¼ teaspoon whole allspice
5 peppercorns   ½ teaspoon salt
         1 medium-size carrot, finely chopped

Combine all ingredients in a saucepan. Heat mixture to boiling over high heat; reduce heat to low and simmer, covered, about 30 minutes. Set aside to cool thoroughly. Store, covered, in the refrigerator until ready to use.
  Marinate game in the marinade at least 2 days before barbecuing. Makes about 3¼ cups marinade.

CALIFORNIA MARINADE

½ cup cooking oil
¼ cup lemon juice
1 tablespoon paprika
2 tablespoons Worcestershire
 sauce

Dash Tabasco sauce
2 tablespoons vinegar
2 teaspoons salt
2 teaspoons sugar
2 cloves garlic, crushed

Put all ingredients in a pint-size, screw-top jar. Cover jar tightly and shake vigorously to mix ingredients well. Store marinade, tightly covered, in the refrigerator until ready to use. Shake or beat well before using. Makes about 1 cup marinade.

WINE MARINADE

½ cup cooking oil
½ cup red or white wine
2 tablespoons grated onion

1 clove garlic, minced
1½ teaspoons salt
Few drops Tabasco sauce

Combine all ingredients in a pint-size, screw-top jar. Cover jar tightly and store in the refrigerator until ready to use. Shake marinade well before using. Makes about 1 cup.

HAWAIIAN MARINADE

¼ cup sugar
1 teaspoon ginger
1 teaspoon dry mustard
1 teaspoon salt

2 tablespoons molasses
¼ cup soy sauce
¼ cup cooking oil
¼ cup water

2 cloves garlic, crushed

Combine all ingredients in a pint-size, screw-top jar. Cover jar and shake vigorously. Store marinade in refrigerator until ready to use. Shake marinade vigorously before using. Makes about 1 cup marinade.

Basting Sauce Selection Chart

Beef Good With
Savory Basting Sauce, p. 126
Jiffy Basting Sauce, p. 125
Wine Basting Sauce, p. 127
Beer Basting Sauce, p. 58

Veal Good With
Vermouth Basting Sauce, p. 125
Savory Basting Sauce, p. 126
Easy Basting Sauce, p. 37
Lime-Ginger Sauce, p. 127

Ham or Pork Good With
Curry Sauce, p. 124
Sweet-Sour Basting Sauce,
 p. 126
Florida Special, p. 126
Jiffy Basting Sauce, p. 125
Beer Basting Sauce, p. 58
Suckling Sauce, p. 65

Lamb Good With
Bar-B-Que Basting Sauce,
 p. 127
Lime-Ginger Sauce, p. 127
Savory Basting Sauce, p. 126

Easy Basting Sauce, p. 37
Curry Sauce, p. 124

Poultry Good With
Vermouth Basting Sauce, p. 125
Roquefort Sauce, p. 125
Florida Special, p. 126
Jiffy Basting Sauce, p. 125
Easy Basting Sauce, p. 37

Fish and Sea Food Good With
Sweet-Sour Basting Sauce,
 p. 126
Roquefort Sauce, p. 125
Bar-B-Que Basting Sauce,
 p. 127
Lime-Ginger Sauce, p. 127
Curry Sauce, p. 124

Game Good With
Florida Special, p. 126
Wine Basting Sauce, p. 127
Easy Basting Sauce, p. 37
Curry Sauce, p. 124
Bar-B-Que Basting Sauce,
 p. 127

CURRY SAUCE

6 tablespoons butter or margarine	1 teaspoon salt
¼ cup flour	⅛ teaspoon pepper
2 teaspoons curry powder	2½ cups hot chicken consommé or chicken stock

Melt butter in a saucepan; remove from heat. Add flour
and next 3 ingredients; stir until smooth. Slowly stir in
hot consommé or stock. Cook and stir until sauce is
slightly thickened. Makes 3 cups.

JIFFY BASTING SAUCE

2 tablespoons cooking oil
1 small onion, minced
1 clove garlic, minced
1 teaspoon dry mustard
1 tablespoon Worcestershire
sauce

½ cup vinegar
¼ cup packed brown sugar
1 can (6 ounces) tomato
paste
Few grains chili powder,
if desired
½ cup water

Combine oil, onion and garlic in a saucepan. Simmer and stir over low heat 5 minutes. Add dry mustard and remaining ingredients. Simmer 10 minutes more, stirring occasionally. Use sauce warm. Makes about 2 cups sauce.

ROQUEFORT SAUCE

½ cup cooking oil
¼ cup crumbled
Roquefort cheese
¼ teaspoon paprika

½ cup lemon juice
¼ teaspoon salt
¼ teaspoon pepper

Put all ingredients in a pint-size, screw-top jar. Cover jar and shake vigorously to mix ingredients well. Store sauce, covered, in the refrigerator until ready to use. Shake or beat sauce well before using. Makes about 1¼ cups sauce.

VERMOUTH BASTING SAUCE

½ cup cooking oil
½ cup dry Vermouth

1 teaspoon salt
⅛ teaspoon pepper

Combine all ingredients in a pint-size, screw-top jar. Cover jar; store in refrigerator until ready to use. Shake sauce well before using. Makes 1 cup.

SAVORY BASTING SAUCE

½ cup sherry wine
¼ cup cooking oil
2 teaspoons onion powder
2 teaspoons brown sugar

1 teaspoon prepared mustard
½ teaspoon thyme
1 teaspoon marjoram
1 teaspoon salt

½ teaspoon black pepper

Put all ingredients in a pint-size, screw-top jar. Cover jar tightly; shake vigorously to mix well. Store sauce, covered, in the refrigerator until ready to use. Shake sauce before using. Makes about ⅔ cup.

FLORIDA SPECIAL

¼ cup cooking oil
⅓ cup vinegar
⅔ cup canned orange or grapefruit juice
2 tablespoons Worcestershire sauce

½ cup catchup
¼ cup minced onion
Dash Tabasco sauce
2½ teaspoons salt
½ teaspoon chili powder
¼ teaspoon oregano

Put all ingredients in a pint-size, screw-top jar. Cover jar and chill until ready to use. Shake or beat sauce well before using. Makes about 1¾ cups sauce.

SWEET-SOUR BASTING SAUCE

2 tablespoons cooking oil
1 teaspoon salt
2 tablespoons minced green pepper
1 clove garlic, peeled

½ cup thawed, frozen pineapple juice concentrate
⅓ cup packed dark brown sugar
½ cup wine vinegar
1 teaspoon soy sauce

Put oil and next 3 ingredients in a small saucepan. Cook and stir 5 minutes. Discard garlic. Add pineapple juice and remaining ingredients. Cook and stir 5 minutes longer. Use sauce warm. Makes about 1½ cups sauce.

LIME-GINGER SAUCE

¼ cup cooking oil
¼ cup vinegar
1 clove garlic, minced
½ teaspoon salt
Dash pepper

½ teaspoon ginger
1 teaspoon rosemary
1 teaspoon grated horse-radish
¼ cup lime juice
½ teaspoon grated lime peel

Put all ingredients in a screw-top jar. Cover jar tightly; shake well. Store sauce in refrigerator until ready to use; shake well before using. Makes about ¾ cup.

BAB-B-QUE BASTING SAUCE

½ cup cooking oil
¾ cup wine vinegar
¼ cup water
2 teaspoons salt

3 tablespoons sugar
1½ teaspoons Tabasco sauce
¼ teaspoon Worcestershire sauce
1 small bay leaf

Combine all ingredients in a small saucepan. Bring to a boil over medium heat. Keep warm by the side of the fire while using. Makes about 1½ cups sauce.

WINE BASTING SAUCE

Put *½ cup red or white wine, ¼ cup cooking oil, ½ teaspoon oregano, 1 clove garlic, crushed* and *1 small bay leaf* in a pint-size, screw-top jar. Cover jar; shake well to mix. Store sauce in refrigerator until ready to use; shake sauce well before using. May also be used as a marinade. Makes about ¾ cup.

Glaze Selection Chart

Beef Good With
Ginger Glaze, p. 129
Honey-Clove Glaze, p. 128

Veal Good With
Currant Glaze, p. 60
Curry Apricot Glaze, p. 71
Banana Orange Glaze, p. 129
Honey-Clove Glaze, p. 128

Ham or Pork Good With
Currant Glaze, p. 60
Apricot Honey Glaze, p. 57
Ginger Glaze, p. 129
Cranberry Glaze, p. 129
Peanut Butter Glaze, p. 129
Pineapple Glaze, p. 130

Lamb Good With
Orange Marmalade Glaze,
　p. 76

Curry Apricot Glaze, p. 71
Ginger Glaze, p. 129

Poultry Good With
Orange Marmalade Glaze,
　p. 76
Ginger Glaze, p. 129
Cranberry Glaze, p. 129
Banana Orange Glaze, p. 129

Fish and Sea Food Good With
Currant Glaze, p. 60
Curry Apricot Glaze, p. 71
Pineapple Glaze, p. 130

Game Good With
Orange Marmalade Glaze,
　p. 76
Cranberry Glaze, p. 129
Peanut Butter Glaze, p. 129
Banana Orange Glaze, p. 129
Honey-Clove Glaze, p. 128

HONEY-CLOVE GLAZE

¼ cup honey
2 tablespoons lemon juice
⅛ teaspoon ground cloves
1 teaspoon soy sauce

Combine all ingredients in
a small, screw-top jar. Stir
to mix well. Use glaze immediately or cover jar and
store in the refrigerator until ready to use. Mix well before using. Makes about ⅓
cup. For a whole ham, in-
crease the amounts 4 times.

CRANBERRY GLAZE

1 cup mashed, jellied cranberry   ¼ teaspoon ginger
   sauce   ¼ teaspoon cinnamon
      ⅓ cup firmly packed brown sugar

Combine all ingredients in a saucepan. Heat and stir until sugar is dissolved. Makes about 1⅓ cups.

PEANUT BUTTER GLAZE

Combine in a small bowl, *¼ cup orange juice, 2 tablespoons homogenized peanut butter and 1½ teaspoons honey;* stir to mix well. Makes about ⅓ cup.

GINGER GLAZE

Water   ½ cup firmly packed
1 can (6 ounces) tomato paste   brown sugar
⅓ cup soy sauce   ¾ teaspoon ginger
      2 or 3 cloves garlic, minced

Combine ⅓ cup water and remaining ingredients in a saucepan. Place over medium heat; cook and stir about 5 minutes adding more water if needed to maintain proper consistency. Use immediately, or store in a tightly covered jar in the refrigerator. Makes about 1½ cups.

BANANA ORANGE GLAZE

1 large fully-ripe banana   1 tablespoon lemon juice
¼ cup thawed, frozen orange   ¼ cup dark corn syrup
   juice concentrate   ⅛ teaspoon salt

Peel banana and put in a bowl. Mash banana with a fork. Stir in remaining ingredients. Makes 1 cup glaze.

PINEAPPLE GLAZE

1 can (8 ounces) crushed   1 teaspoon dry mustard
   pineapple   Juice of 1 lemon
1 cup firmly packed brown sugar   Dash of salt
1 tablespoon prepared mustard

Drain the syrup from the pineapple and set aside. Combine the drained pineapple with the sugar, prepared and dry mustard, lemon juice and salt in a saucepan. Heat and stir until sugar dissolves. Add as much of the reserved syrup as is necessary to make a mixture of good brushing consistency. Makes about 1½ cups glaze.

Note: If a blender is available combine all ingredients in container and blend until smooth. Do not heat.

Barbecue Sauce Selection Chart

Beef Good With
Tangy Barbecue Sauce, p. 133
Onion Sauce, p. 132
Red Hot Barbecue Sauce, p. 131
Horse-radish Sauce, p. 131
Fiesta Sauce, p. 53

Veal Good With
Red Devil Dip, p. 133
Tangy Barbecue Sauce, p. 133
Onion Sauce, p. 132
Fiesta Sauce, p. 53
Glossy Cherry Sauce, p. 132

Ham or Pork Good With
Glossy Cherry Sauce, p. 132
Red Hot Barbecue Sauce, p. 131
Horse-radish Sauce, p. 131
Fiesta Sauce, p. 53

Lamb Good With
Red Devil Dip, p. 133
Ranch Barbecue Sauce, p. 131

Lemon Sauce, p. 133
Onion Sauce, p. 132
Fiesta Sauce, p. 53

Poultry Good With
Ranch Barbecue Sauce, p. 131
Lemon Sauce, p. 133
Glossy Cherry Sauce, p. 132
Red Hot Barbecue Sauce, p. 131

Fish and Sea Food Good With
Ranch Barbecue Sauce, p. 131
Red Devil Dip, p. 133
Lemon Sauce, p. 133
Tangy Barbecue Sauce, p. 133
Red Hot Barbecue Sauce, p. 131

Game Good With
Glossy Cherry Sauce, p. 132
Onion Sauce, p. 132
Horse-radish Sauce, p. 131
Fiesta Sauce, p. 53
Lemon Sauce, p. 133

RANCH BARBECUE SAUCE

1 cup mayonnaise
1 can (6 ounces) tomato paste
¼ cup wine vinegar
3 tablespoons Worcestershire sauce

1 tablespoon chopped onion
1½ tablespoons prepared horse-radish
1½ teaspoons salt
½ teaspoon pepper
¼ teaspoon Tabasco sauce

Combine all ingredients in a small bowl; blend well. Use immediately or refrigerate in a screw-top jar until ready to use. Makes 2 cups sauce.

Note: This sauce may also be used as a basting sauce.

HORSE-RADISH SAUCE

¼ cup salad dressing
1½ tablespoons prepared horse-radish

½ teaspoon salt
Dash Tabasco sauce
1 teaspoon prepared mustard

⅓ cup heavy cream, whipped

Combine salad dressing and next 4 ingredients; stir to mix well. Gently fold whipped cream into salad dressing mixture. Store in refrigerator until ready to use. Makes about 1 cup sauce.

RED HOT BARBECUE SAUCE

¼ cup molasses
¼ cup prepared mustard
¼ cup firmly packed brown sugar

¾ cup vinegar
½ cup canned pineapple juice
¼ cup Worcestershire sauce
½ teaspoon Tabasco sauce

Put molasses, mustard and brown sugar into a small bowl; stir to mix well. Add remaining ingredients; mix well. Makes about 2 cups sauce.

GLOSSY CHERRY SAUCE

1 can (1 pound) unsweetened cherries	¼ cup lemon juice
	1 teaspoon grated lemon peel
Water	⅛ teaspoon salt
1 tablespoon cornstarch	½ teaspoon cinnamon
2 tablespoons melted butter	¼ cup sugar

Few drops red food coloring, if desired

Drain cherries and measure juice. Set cherries aside. Add enough water to cherry juice to make 1½ cups liquid. Blend ¼ cup of the liquid with cornstarch in a small bowl.

In a saucepan, combine all the ingredients except cherries. Bring mixture to a boil; slowly add and stir in reserved cornstarch mixture. Cook and stir sauce until thickened. Add cherries; simmer about 5 minutes, stirring occasionally. Stir in food coloring. Serve sauce hot. Makes about 2½ cups.

ONION SAUCE

1 tablespoon butter or margarine	2 beef bouillon cubes
2 tablespoons sugar	1 cup boiling water
2 medium-size onions, sliced	1 tablespoon vinegar
1 tablespoon flour	Salt, to taste

Melt butter in a skillet; stir in sugar. Separate onion slices into rings and put in melted butter. Cook onion over low heat, stirring often, until almost tender but not brown. Remove from heat. Sprinkle flour over onions and toss gently to moisten. Dissolve bouillon cubes in boiling water and slowly add and stir into onion mixture. Return sauce to medium heat; bring to a boil, stirring constantly. Reduce heat to low; cook and stir until sauce is slightly thickened and smooth or, about 5 minutes. Add and stir in vinegar and salt; serve hot. Makes about 2 cups sauce.

RED DEVIL DIP

¼ cup butter or margarine
2 teaspoons onion powder
2 tablespoons Worcestershire sauce
½ teaspoon pepper
¼ cup chili sauce
⅓ cup prepared mustard
Curry powder, to taste

Melt butter in a saucepan. Stir in onion powder, Worcestershire sauce, pepper, chili sauce and mustard. Simmer over low heat until well blended. Stir in curry powder. Serve hot or cold. Makes about ½ cup sauce.

LEMON BARBECUE SAUCE

1 clove of garlic, crushed
½ teaspoon salt
½ teaspoon pepper
⅛ teaspoon ginger
2 tablespoons chopped onion
¼ cup olive oil
½ cup lemon juice

Combine all ingredients in a screw-top jar. Cover jar and shake well. Allow sauce to stand overnight to blend flavors. Makes about ¾ cup sauce.

TANGY BARBECUE SAUCE

1 can (6 ounces) tomato paste
1 teaspoon dry mustard
¼ cup firmly packed brown sugar
1 teaspoon salt
Few grains chili powder
1 tablespoon Worcestershire sauce
1 medium-size onion, minced
¼ cup wine vinegar
2 tablespoons water
2 teaspoons lemon juice

Combine all ingredients in a saucepan. Heat to boiling, stirring occasionally. Remove from heat; let stand several hours at room temperature to blend the flavors before serving. Makes about 1¼ cups.

RELISH "FIXINS"

Are you looking for some tidbit appetizers or meat accompaniments? Here they are! You can make them from anything from canned fruits to raw vegetables. Just remember, almost all relishes are improved if you prepare and chill them ahead of time.

HARVEST RELISH

1 cup chopped unpared apples
¾ cup shredded cabbage
½ cup minced celery
1 tablespoon chopped green pepper
4 teaspoons chopped pimiento
⅓ cup sugar
3 tablespoons vinegar
½ teaspoon salt
¼ teaspoon ground allspice

Put the apples and next 4 ingredients in a bowl. Combine sugar and remaining ingredients in another bowl; stir to mix well. Pour sugar-spice mixture over apple mixture; toss to mix well. Spoon apple relish into a pint-size, screw-top jar; cover tightly. Makes 1 pint.

PINK PICKLED PEACHES

1 can (30 ounces) peach halves
½ cup cider vinegar
2 tablespoons red cinnamon candies
½ cup sugar
⅛ teaspoon ground allspice
1 piece stick cinnamon, about 3 inches long
Whole cloves

Drain peach halves; reserve 1 cup of the syrup. Set peaches aside. Combine the 1 cup syrup with the vinegar and next 4 ingredients in a saucepan. Simmer mixture 3 or 4 minutes to dissolve sugar and blend flavors.

Stud each peach half with 4 or 5 cloves. Put peaches into a screw-top jar. Pour syrup on top. Cool and cover jar tightly. Refrigerate until ready to use.

TOMATO AND PEPPER RELISH

1 cup chopped tomatoes	2 tablespoons vinegar
¼ cup minced celery	1 teaspoon salt
⅓ cup minced green pepper	¼ teaspoon dry mustard
⅓ cup minced onion	2 tablespoons cooking oil

Put the tomatoes, celery, green pepper and onion into a bowl; drain slightly. Combine vinegar, salt, mustard and cooking oil in a small bowl. Pour over tomato mixture; toss to mix well. Spoon the relish into a pint-size, screw-top jar; cover tightly. Store jar in refrigerator 2 or 3 days before using. Makes 1 pint.

CUCUMBER RELISH

1¾ cups minced cucumber	2 teaspoons salt
½ cup grated carrot	¼ cup vinegar
¼ cup minced onion	¾ teaspoon dill seeds

Combine all ingredients in a bowl. Toss to mix well. Spoon the relish into a screw-top jar. Cover jar and chill in refrigerator overnight to blend flavors. Makes about 1 pint relish.

GREEN CABBAGE RELISH

1 cup finely chopped green cabbage	¼ cup minced celery
	½ teaspoon caraway seeds
¼ cup grated carrot	1 teaspoon salt
¼ cup minced onion	⅓ cup vinegar

Combine all ingredients in a bowl. Toss to mix well. Spoon relish into a large, screw-top jar. Cover jar and chill thoroughly to blend flavors. Makes about 1 pint relish.

CORN RELISH

3 tablespoons diced green pepper   ½ cup chopped celery
2 tablespoons chopped pimiento   ½ teaspoon salt
2 tablespoons minced onion   ⅓ cup French Dressing
1 can (12 ounces) whole   (see page 138)
    kernel corn, drained   1 tablespoon vinegar

Combine all ingredients in a bowl; toss to mix well. Put mixture into a screw-top jar and refrigerate until ready to use. Makes about 1 pint.

SHARP 'N' SPICY RELISH

2 cups chopped cooked beets   1 cup sugar
2 cups chopped green cabbage   1½ tablespoons salt
⅓ to ½ cup prepared   1 teaspoon mustard seeds
    horse-radish   1 cup vinegar

Combine all ingredients in a bowl. Toss to mix well. Spoon relish into a large, screw-top jar; cover tightly and refrigerate. Makes about 1 quart relish.

MINT-PICKLED CARROTS

4 or 5 medium-size carrots   ½ cup water
½ cup vinegar   1 tablespoon dry mint flakes
            3 tablespoons sugar

Wash and scrape the carrots; cut into sticks and set aside. Combine vinegar and remaining ingredients in a saucepan; stir to mix well. Put the carrot sticks in vinegar mixture. Place saucepan over high heat and bring liquid to a boil; boil, covered, about 2 minutes. Lift carrots out of liquid and pack in a pint-size, screw-top jar. Pour liquid over carrots. Cool and cover jar tightly. Refrigerate until ready to use. Makes 1 pint.

ABOUT SALADS AND DESSERTS

Salads and desserts put the finishing touches on a barbecue! Plan your menu carefully so they compliment the meal. For a patio barbecue, with a refrigerator practically at your elbow, you can make salads or desserts as elaborate as you like. But, if the gang has decided to go to the beach, keep foods simple. Perishable foods won't stand the rigors of a trip to the beach or picnic grounds, especially if the day is hot and the trip is long. Finger foods, on a picnic, cut down on the amount of carting and are easy to eat. (Additional hints on planning may be found on page 149.) Elaborate as well as simple recipes for salads and desserts are on the following pages for your selection.

THE TOSSED SALAD

Tops among salads with men and women too, is the tossed salad. Some of the greens to use are iceberg lettuce, Boston lettuce, escarole, romaine, endive, water cress, cabbage, spinach, young beet and mustard greens.

For a basic tossed green salad, select one, two or more kinds of greens. Wash them thoroughly and drain well; put in a plastic bag and place in the crisper to chill. When you are ready to serve the salad, rub the salad bowl with a cut clove of garlic; tear or cut the crisp greens into bite-size pieces and put into the bowl. Drizzle a well-seasoned salad dressing over the greens. Remember, not too much dressing, you'll want just enough to coat the leaves. Then, toss the greens lightly; every leaf should be coated with dressing. Serve at once!

There are innumerable ways of varying the tossed green salad. For color and flavor, you may add canned or raw vegetables, fruit, cheese, eggs, olives, meat, fish, sea food, croutons, potato chips, even nuts. In other words be as daring as you like, the tossed salad can be the appetizer, enhance the main dish or, be the star of the meal; it all depends upon what you add to the greens.

SALAD DRESSINGS

French Dressing

Combine ¾ *cup olive oil, ¼ cup wine vinegar, 1 teaspoon salt, ¼ teaspoon pepper* and *¾ teaspoon paprika* in a cruet or screw-top jar. Shake well before using. Makes 1 cup.

Honey Dressing

Combine ½ *cup strained honey, ¼ cup hot water, ¼ cup lemon juice, ¼ cup olive oil, ¼ teaspoon salt* and *¼ teaspoon ginger;* beat with a rotary beater. Store in a cruet or screw-top jar. Shake well before using. Makes about 1¼ cups.

Roquefort Dressing

Put *2 ounces of Roquefort or blue cheese* and *2 to 4 tablespoons vinegar* in a bowl; blend with a fork. Add *¼ teaspoon dry mustard, ¼ teaspoon salt* and *a dash Tabasco sauce.* Add and stir in *1 cup sour cream;* beat until smooth. Add *½ cup mayonnaise* and continue to beat until well blended. Makes about 1¾ cups.

FRUITED CABBAGE

4½ cups finely shredded green cabbage
¾ cup seedless white grapes
¾ cup chopped red unpared apples
½ cup mayonnaise
3 tablespoons lemon juice
½ teaspoon grated lemon peel
2 tablespoons sugar
¾ teaspoon salt
1 teaspoon prepared mustard
½ teaspoon celery seeds

Combine cabbage, grapes and apples in a large bowl. In a small bowl, put mayonnaise and remaining ingredients; stir to mix well. Pour mayonnaise mixture over cabbage mixture; toss to mix well. Chill well. Turn into a lettuce lined bowl and garnish, if desired, with red-skinned apple slices. Makes about 5 cups.

CUCUMBER-ALMOND SALAD

2 cucumbers, pared and thinly sliced
½ teaspoon salt
1 cup sour cream
⅓ cup slivered almonds
1 tablespoon minced onion
1½ teaspoons lime juice
Salt and pepper to taste

Combine cucumbers and the ½ teaspon salt. Let stand about 15 minutes; drain. In a bowl, combine sour cream and remaining ingredients; pour over cucumbers and toss. Chill well. Makes 6 servings.

RANCHER'S MUSHROOMS

Select large, firm mushrooms; cut lengthwise, into thin slices. Sprinkle a little chopped parsley over mushrooms. Pour enough French Dressing (see page 138) over mushrooms to cover; marinate at least 1 hour. To serve, spoon drained mushrooms onto water cress.

ZUCCHINI QUICKY

Arrange precooked, drained zucchini on lettuce. Serve with French Dressing (see recipe on page 138).

HEARTY PICNIC SALAD

4 cups cooked elbow
macaroni, chilled
1 can (1 pound) kidney
beans, drained
4 frankfurters, sliced thin
1 cup mayonnaise
½ cup chili sauce

Salt and pepper, to taste
Few drops Tabasco sauce
1 tablespoon prepared
horse-radish
1 teaspoon prepared mustard
1 teaspoon Worcestershire
sauce

Crisp salad greens

Combine macaroni, beans and frankfurters. Combine mayonnaise and next 6 ingredients. Pour mayonnaise mixture over macaroni; toss to mix well. Chill. Turn into a bowl lined with salad greens. Makes 8 servings.

HOT POTATO SALAD

¼ cup sour cream
¼ cup mayonnaise
2 teaspoons salt
¼ teaspoon black pepper
4 cups hot, diced potatoes
½ cup diced cucumber

½ cup chopped celery
2 tablespoons minced stuffed
olives
1 green pepper, diced
1 dill pickle, minced
1 tablespoon minced parsley

8 slices crisp bacon, crumbled

Combine sour cream and next 3 ingredients in a small bowl. In a large bowl, put potatoes and next 6 ingredients; add sour cream mixture. Toss the salad carefully to mix well. Spoon salad into a heatproof dish; garnish with bacon. Keep salad warm. Makes 6 to 8 servings.

SUNSHINE POTATO SALAD

4 cups diced, cold cooked
  potatoes
1 small onion, chopped
2 tablespoons chopped
  parsley

1 cup chopped celery
1 teaspoon salt
Mustard Salad Dressing (see
  recipe below)
Crisp lettuce

Combine potatoes, onion, parsley, celery and salt. Add
Mustard Salad Dressing; toss salad gently to mix well.
Chill about 1 hour. Turn salad into a lettuce lined salad
bowl. Makes 6 to 8 servings.

MUSTARD SALAD DRESSING

4 tablespoons prepared mustard
2 tablespoons light cream
2 tablespoons sugar

2 tablespoons vinegar
1/4 teaspoon salt
Dash pepper

Combine all ingredients; beat with a rotary beater until
light and fluffy. Makes about 2/3 cup.

THE FRUIT SALAD

A well-arranged bowl or platter of fresh, canned and/or thawed frozen fruits is always a refreshing treat! Make it the appetizer, accompaniment to the main course, or the dessert.

The "mix-your-own" fruit salad is fun to arrange and gives your guests a choice of fruits. Be sure to chill the fruits and the bowl well ahead of time. Use such fruits as spears or balls of watermelon, cantaloupe and honeydew; spears or chunks of pineapple, bananas, mangos, wedges of apples, pears and peaches; sections of oranges, tangerines and grapefruit. Whole berries and grapes are also good additions to the salad.

Just before serving, line a salad bowl with crisp greens. Mound cottage cheese in center of the bowl, if desired. Cut and arrange the fruits, as shown above. (To prevent bananas, peaches and apples from darkening, dip in lemon juice.) Serve salad with small bowls of several kinds of dressings on the side.

FROSTED FUDGE BARS

1 cup sifted cake flour	2 eggs
¼ teaspoon baking powder	1 cup sugar
¼ teaspoon salt	½ teaspoon vanilla
½ cup butter or margarine	1 cup broken walnuts
2 squares (1 ounce each)	Bittersweet Frosting
unsweetened chocolate	(see page 148)

½ cup chopped walnuts

Set the oven for moderate, 350°F. Grease an 8-inch square pan.

Sift together the flour, baking powder and salt; set aside. Melt butter and chocolate together over hot water. Meanwhile, beat eggs; gradually beat in sugar. Beat until well blended. Add and stir in melted chocolate mixture and vanilla; beat hard 1 minute. Add sifted dry ingredients, a little at a time; stir well after each addition. Stir in the broken nuts; turn into prepared pan. Bake 35 to 40 minutes, or until top is dry. Cool in pan, on a wire rack, just until bottom feels warm. Spread with Bittersweet Frosting; sprinkle with the ½ cup chopped nuts. When frosting is set, cut into bars 4 x 1-inches wide. Makes about 16.

LEMON COCONUT CAKE

2 cups sifted cake flour	1 teaspoon vanilla
3 teaspoons baking powder	⅔ cup milk
½ teaspoon salt	Lemon Filling (see below)
5 egg whites	Fluffy White Frosting
½ cup shortening	(see page 148)
1⅓ cups sugar	Moist-pack shredded coconut

Set oven for moderately hot, 375°F. Grease two round 8-inch cake pans. Sift together the flour, baking powder and salt. Whip egg whites until stiff but not dry.

Cream shortening well; gradually beat in sugar. Beat until well blended. Stir in vanilla. Add sifted dry ingredients alternately with milk, a little at a time, stirring only until smooth after each addition. Gently fold in whipped egg whites. Turn batter into pans. Bake 25 to 30 minutes or, until cake springs back when lightly touched with fingertip. Cool cake slightly, 10 to 15 minutes, in pans on a rack. Remove from pans; cool.

Spread Lemon Filling between layers. Cover tops and sides with frosting; sprinkle with coconut.

Lemon Filling

Mix together *½ cup sugar* and *¼ cup flour;* gradually add *1 cup warm water.* Stir in *3 well-beaten egg yolks.* Cook over hot water until thick; stir constantly. Cover; cook 5 minutes longer. Remove from heat; add *2 teaspoons grated lemon peel, juice of 1 lemon* and *2 tablespoons butter or margarine.* Mix well, cool.

MARBLE CAKE

1¾ cups sifted cake flour	2 eggs, well beaten
2 teaspoons baking powder	1 teaspoon vanilla
½ teaspoon salt	½ cup milk
½ cup shortening	1 square (1 ounce) unsweetened chocolate, melted
1 cup sugar	2 tablespoons milk

Bittersweet Frosting (see page 148)

Set oven for moderate, 350°F. Grease an 8-inch square cake pan well.

Sift together flour, baking powder and salt. Set aside. Cream shortening thoroughly; gradually beat in sugar and continue beating until well blended. Add eggs and vanilla and beat well. Add sifted dry ingredients alternately with the ½ cup milk, a little at a time and stir only until smooth after each addition.

Divide batter into 2 parts. Combine chocolate and remaining 2 tablespoons milk. Stir chocolate into 1 part of batter blending well. Drop alternate spoonfuls of light and dark batters into the cake pan. Bake 50 to 60 minutes or, until cake springs back when lightly touched with fingertip. Let stand in pan on a rack 10 to 15 minutes. Remove cake from pan; cool on rack. Frost with Bittersweet Frosting.

BANANA CUP CAKES

Use a packaged white or gold cake mix whose mixing directions specify the addition of 1 cup liquid, either water or milk, and substitute 1½ cups mashed bananas for the liquid. Or, when packaged mix directions specify 1 cup water plus eggs, add required number of eggs but reduce the water to ½ cup and add 1 cup mashed bananas. Mix cake batter as directed on package. Divide batter among cup cake pans; bake as directed on package. Cool cakes slightly, about 10 minutes, in pans on a wire rack. Remove from pans; cool.

When cakes are cool, cut a cone-shaped piece out of each top. Fill with a frosting from page 148 or, the Lemon Filling on page 145. Put the cone-shaped piece back in place. Wrap at once with no fear of losing half of the filling on the wrappings.

MOLASSES WALNUT COOKIES

3½ cups sifted all-purpose flour	1 cup firmly packed brown sugar
½ teaspoon salt	½ cup molasses
1 teaspoon baking soda	3 tablespoons water
¾ cup shortening	2 eggs, well beaten
½ cup chopped walnuts	

Sift together flour, salt and baking soda; set aside. Cream shortening in a bowl; slowly add and beat in sugar. Continue beating until well blended and fluffy. Stir molasses and water into batter. Add eggs; beat well. Add sifted dry ingredients and walnuts, a little at a time, to egg mixture. Blend well after each addition. Cover bowl and chill well, about 2 hours.

Set oven for hot, 400°F. Grease cooky sheets. Drop dough by tablespoonfuls on cooky sheets, about 2 inches apart. Bake 10 to 12 minutes. Remove from pans and cool on wire racks. Makes about 5 dozen cookies.

PEANUT BUTTER COOKIES

1½ cups sifted all-purpose flour	½ cup peanut butter
¼ teaspoon salt	2 eggs, well beaten
½ teaspoon baking soda	¼ cup milk
1 teaspoon cinnamon	1 teaspoon vanilla
¼ cup shortening	¾ cup seedless raisins
1 cup sugar	¾ cup rolled oats

Sift together flour and next 3 ingredients; set aside. Cream shortening thoroughly in a bowl; gradually beat in sugar. Beat until well blended. Add peanut butter; blend well. Stir in eggs, milk and vanilla; mix thoroughly. Add sifted dry ingredients, a little at a time, stirring until blended after each addition. Mix in raisins and rolled oats. Cover bowl; chill about 1 hour.

Set oven for moderate, 350°F. Drop dough by teaspoonfuls on ungreased cooky sheets, about 2 inches apart. Bake cookies 15 minutes or until golden brown. Remove from sheets; cool on racks. Makes about 4 dozen.

FRUIT BARS

¾ cup sifted all-purpose flour	¼ cup shortening,
½ teaspoon baking powder	melted
½ teaspoon salt	2 eggs, well beaten
1 cup firmly packed brown sugar	1 cup chopped nuts
1 cup chopped pitted dates	

Set the oven for moderate, 350°F. Grease an 8-inch square pan.

Sift together flour, baking powder and salt into a mixing bowl. Add brown sugar and stir to mix well. Mix melted shortening with eggs and add to sifted dry ingredients. Stir batter just until mixed. Stir in nuts and dates. Turn into greased pan. Bake 30 minutes or until top is dry and edges are slightly brown. Cut into bars while warm. Makes about 16 bars.

LAZY SUSAN SUNDAES

Serve ice cream and sherbets "lazy-susan" style for your next barbecue. With one or more kinds of store-bought or homemade ice cream and a tray chock-full of bowls of toppers, the simple ice cream dessert becomes a dazzling sundae. Fill the bowls with fruits such as sliced peaches, bananas, strawberries, etc., miniature marshmallows, nuts, sauces, whipped cream and cherries! You might even include cantaloupe melons, cut in half, for those who want a super-special sundae.

BITTERSWEET FROSTING

Melt *2 squares (1 ounce each) unsweetened chocolate* over hot water. Combine *¼ cup sugar* and *3 tablespoons water* in a small saucepan. Heat and stir over medium heat until sugar dissolves; boil 1 minute. Pour sugar slowly into the melted chocolate, stirring constantly. Beat chocolate mixture until thick. Add and stir in *½ teaspoon vanilla*. Enough frosting for top of one, 8-inch square cake or a pan of Fudge Bars.

FLUFFY WHITE FROSTING

Combine *1 cup sugar, ⅓ cup water,* and *1 teaspoon vinegar* in a saucepan. Place over moderate heat; stir until sugar dissolves. Boil without stirring to 236°F. on a candy thermometer or, until syrup spins a thread when dropped from the tip of a spoon. Whip *2 egg whites* until stiff but not dry. Pour hot syrup slowly over egg whites, beating constantly with a rotary or electric beater. Continue beating until frosting holds its shape. Stir in *½ teaspoon vanilla*. Frosts top and sides of one, 8-inch layer cake.

MEMOS TO THE HOST

A barbecue or cookout, as close to the kitchen as the backyard patio or, as far away as the beach or state park, is becoming more popular each year. As a casual get together it's a wonderful way to let everyone from 2 to 80 get in the act. And, if those supplying the chow have a little planning "know how", it's even better! So, if you're elected to this post, take a few minutes to read the following paragraphs.

A menu must always fit the occasion. Thus, before planning one, take into consideration where and when the barbecue will take place. Remember, the weather is an important factor. On a hot summer's day foods requiring little preparation are in demand. While on a cool day, everyone will want to crowd 'round the fire.

Take stock of your cooking and serving facilities. The type barbecue and serving equipment you have will control, to a great extent, the number of people you can serve and the type menu. But, auxiliary equipment such as kebob skewers, pots and pans, hand grills and just plain aluminum foil can do an extraordinary job of increasing the cooking capacity of any unit. Browse through the chapters on Kebobs, Hand Grills and Barbecued Extras for recipe ideas using these aids.

Next, consider the age range of the guests and their eating preferences, when possible. But, if you don't know their personal preferences, it's a good idea to stick to the simpler foods. Serve sauces, relishes, etc. to add interest to the menu.

149

You're now ready to get down to the actual menu planning. Keep these few basic rules in mind:

1. Generally speaking, a buffet or help-yourself menu is the most popular kind. It gives the host more free time to mingle with the guests and makes for a more informal, get-acquainted type party.

2. Keep the menu simple and serve foods easy to handle. Meat, a salad, one or two vegetables if it's a dinner, a bread and dessert make ample fare for any barbecue. Unless you're serving hot dogs and hamburgers, one kind of meat is plenty. Dress up the meat with a glaze or, serve relish or sauce accompaniments, if you like.

3. Have plenty of food. Remember, everyone eats more out-of-doors. A good rule to follow when ordering meat is to figure on 1½ to 2 servings per person. For each serving, allow ¼ to ⅓ pound solid meat with little or no fat (ie. ground round steak); ⅓ to ½ pound boneless but fatty meat; ½ to ¾ pound bone-in meat such as rib and leg roasts; 1 pound of very boney meat such as spareribs and chuck steaks; ½ chicken or 1 to 2 chops.

A Backyard Barbecue

A backyard or patio barbecue is the easiest of all. Since it's usually handy to the kitchen facilities, you don't need to be concerned with packing and transporting foods and equipment. So, to keep your trips to the kitchen at a minimum, here are some suggestions.

1. Prepare everything possible ahead of time. Store in sealed air-tight containers, self-sealing type wrap, aluminum foil or plastic bags until ready to use.

2. Casserole or heatproof dishes are just the thing for hot potato salad and other accompaniments. Keep them warm on the side of the barbecue unit. Then, pop them on the buffet table the last minute.

3. Salads such as macaroni are improved by chilling, so prepare and chill several hours before serving.

4. A clothes basket is excellent for carting out all the serving equipment in one trip.

5. When serving a group, keep one bowl of each food in reserve for "seconds".

6. At a buffet for 25 or more, put 2 small bowls or platters of each food on the table, instead of 1 large one. Serve from both sides of the table.

Away From Home Barbecue

A beach, park or roadside barbecue is always controlled by the amount of equipment you can transport and the immediate facilities. Read these suggestions below, then add your own ingenuity as required by the occasion.

1. Keep hot foods hot and cold foods cold. For short trips, heatproof dishes popped out of the oven just before leaving and wrapped in layers of newspaper keep food surprisingly hot. Use small portable ice boxes or vacuum jugs. If you have a freezer at home, freeze the meat and let it thaw on the way. If the trip's a long one, keep food wrapped in foil or layers of newspaper and put in a corrugated box until you get there. Then, let it thaw. Tuck packages of frozen foods between other foods to keep them cool.

2. Place pieces of waxed paper between each hamburger before wrapping. They'll separate easier later.

3. Use paper freezer containers for carting extras.

4. Individual foil-wrapped packs, cooked directly on the coals and just handed to the customers are another must. See chapter on Barbecued Extras.

5. Try a hobo-style meal for a really fast and easy trick (see page 106).

6. Carry milk in a thermos jug or in individual ½ pint containers placed between cartons of frozen foods. And, bottled soft drinks in small or individual-size bottles can also make serving easier.

SPECIAL BARBECUE PARTIES

Cooking outdoors for large numbers has long been a part of the American scene. Originally each region of the country had its traditional way of cooking for a crowd; down East it was the clam bake, the South had its fish fry, the Middlewest was famous for its chicken barbecue, the Southwest is noted for pit barbecuing and the West Coast adopted as its own, the colorful luau from Hawaii. The occasion of many of these get togethers originally was, and frequently still is, an event of community interest such as a political rally, a rodeo, a county fair or a church social.

But with the trend toward outdoor living, these shindigs are now one of the favorite ways of entertaining, whether it's a party for ten or an elaborate affair for a hundred or more. And you don't have to live in Texas to have a pit barbecue or in Massachusetts for a clam bake. All of these special methods of outdoor cooking can be adapted to any locale providing you have sufficient space for cooking and serving the crowd.

Granted, any one of these parties may take more planning, time and effort than the usual type of dinner for the same number of people. But the pleasure and satisfaction to guests and host alike will be worth all the effort required.

Of course, it is necessary to make complete plans well in advance. Have every aspect of the party well planned and organized: the equipment and tools needed, enough food for the crowd, the correct type pit for the fire, right kind and quantity of fuel, sufficient number of people to prepare and assist in serving the food, adequate tables and space for serving and eating, plenty of plates, cups and eating utensils and last of all a plan for the clean-up afterward.

PIT BARBECUES

There are two types of pit barbecues, open pit and deep or closed pit. An open pit is used for cooking a whole animal and it is a shallow one. The meat is cooked directly over the coals and the process is similar to roasting or broiling.

For deep pit barbecuing, meat is cut in large pieces or chunks. It is securely wrapped and tied in packages and put into the pit over live coals then completely buried under earth for the entire cooking time, making the process similar to steaming or Dutch oven cooking.

Hardwood, thoroughly dried, is the preferred fuel to use although you can use charcoal briquets if wood is not available. Some of the woods most frequently used are oak, mesquite, ironwood and any fruit or nut wood such as orange, apple and hickory. You get the best fire if logs are not more than 4 inches thick. So, split them, if necessary.

Procedures for preparing the pit and the meat and for building the fire depends on the particular kind of barbecuing you do.

Open Pit Barbecuing

Open pit barbecuing is the method usually used for cooking a whole young pig, calf or lamb. The pit must be 15 to 18 inches deep, slightly wider and longer than the animal after it is trussed onto the rods plus additional space for maintaining an auxiliary fire. Or, if you prefer, you can dig a second smaller pit for this purpose. This auxiliary fire provides hot coals to add to the main fire for an even cooking temperature.

Select a carcass of first quality meat weighing 40 to 50 pounds, dressed weight. Have the head cut off close to the body and the feet at the first joint. Saw the backbone, lengthwise on the inside, so the animal will lie flat, taking care not to cut the carcass in two.

Use two iron rods about 24 inches longer than the length of the pit. Run these rods parallel to the backbone into the shoulders underneath the rib bones and on through the loins just under the skin. Then, insert several lighter weight rods, crosswise, at intervals through the animal and fasten them to the main rods with bailing wire. These lighter rods prevent meat from falling off the thinner parts of the carcass as it cooks.

Start the fire well in advance of cooking so the bed of coals is about 4 inches deep. Place the meat over the pit, cut-side down, with the ends of the long rods resting on the ground at the ends of the pit, until the meat is well seared. Then, turn the meat over and swab or baste the cut-side with a basting sauce. (You can use Suckling Sauce on page 65. Make about 3 times the recipe for a 40 pound roast.) After basting turn the meat, cut-side down. Continue to cook, cut-side down, turning it over to baste it, as often as necessary, to prevent the meat from getting dry. As meat cooks, add coals from the auxiliary fire as required.

When the meat is almost done, heap coals under the thicker parts and continue to cook until the meat is very tender. Then level the coals with a rake; turn the meat over to brown the skin side. When the skin is crisp and brown, remove the meat from the fire, carve and serve at once. It takes 4 to 6 hours to barbecue a whole carcass, depending on the weight and kind of meat.

Deep Pit Barbecuing

This method of barbecuing is suitable for cooking for as few as 20 or as many as 2000 if you have that many people to feed. The size of the pit required depends on the quantity of meat you have to cook, so before you begin to dig you'll have to do a little estimating.

You will need to allow at least one pound of meat for each person. The meat must be cut in pieces of approximately the same size but the size can range from 6 to 20 pounds per piece. Each piece will have three wrappings, one of foil or parchment, one of muslin and one of burlap. In the pit there must be several inches of space around all sides of each package of meat for circulation of heat during cooking. It is easier to handle the whole operation if the pit is no wider than 3 feet. With these considerations dig the pit from 1½ to 3 feet wide, 3½ feet deep and as long as necessary to accommodate the packaged meat.

Line the entire bottom of the pit and half way up sides with bricks or large, rounded, hard, dry stones. Never use porous or wet stones; they may explode when subjected to heat. Start the fire in the pit far enough ahead of cooking time so you have a bed of ashes about a foot deep. This takes about 3 hours.

Because deep pit barbecuing is moist cooking, less tender cuts of meat, such as shoulder and rump, cook satisfactorily. How you season the meat and the seasonings you use depend on personal preference. You can sprinkle seasonings over the meat—salt, pepper, dry mustard, garlic, onion or seasoned salt, sugar, bay leaf. You might want to marinate it for several hours or even inject a marinade into the meat with a meat syringe. Wrap each piece of meat separately, first in aluminum foil or water-soaked parchment, then in muslin. Next, wrap each roll in a piece of clean burlap and tie the bundle securely with light wire. Have an additional piece of heavy wire for each bundle. Attach one end to the wire tied around the bundle; leave the other end free. This will serve as a handle for lifting. Now dunk all the bundles into a tub of water or spray them with a hose to wet them thoroughly.

When the bed of coals is ready, cover it with about an inch of heated dry sand. Put in the packages of meat and cover the meat with dirt until the hole is completely filled. Work quickly to fill and seal the pit before too much heat escapes. Keep a watchful eye on the dirt covering the pit all during the cooking. If steam seeps out of small holes, cover them with dirt and step on them carefully to seal the holes.

It takes about 5 hours for 6- to 10-pound pieces of beef to cook or 10 to 12 hours for 20-pound pieces.

CHICKEN BARBECUE

The pit for a chicken barbecue really isn't a pit at all but a huge grill built above the ground made of cement or cinder blocks which measure 8 by 8 by 16 inches. These blocks are stacked, three high, without the use of mortar, to make the pit 2 feet high.

For a pit large enough to barbecue chicken for 50 people, you will need a pit 6½ cement blocks long and 3½ blocks wide. The inside measurement of the pit will be about 3 by 7½ feet and requires 54 cement blocks to build. You must also have a piece of half-inch wire mesh, 3 feet wide and 9 feet long, and in addition, 9 pieces of one-inch iron pipe, each about 4½ feet long.

After the blocks are put in place, drive two pieces of the pipe into the ground upright at the outside corners at one end of the pit. Roll one end of the wire mesh around another piece of pipe 2 or 3 times and fasten it securely with wire. Now lay the pipe, with wire mesh attached, across the end of the pit and brace it by fastening it securely to the uprights. Leave the wire mesh rolled up until the fire is built.

Use charcoal briquets for the fire. It takes about 50 pounds for 50 people. Scatter wood shavings in the pit and dampen them slightly with kerosene. Then cover the shavings with charcoal and light. Allow time for the smoke to burn off and the charcoal to become hot enough for cooking, about 15 to 30 minutes.

Lay the remaining pieces of iron pipe across the pit at regular intervals and unroll the wire mesh. This wire supported by the pipe makes a grid for cooking.

Chickens weighing from 2½ to 3 pounds, dressed

weight, are the ideal size. They should be split in two and will barbecue more evenly if the backbone and neck are removed. If you prefer, you can use chickens weighing up to 5 pounds. These larger chickens should be cut in quarters. Allow a half or quarter chicken per person, depending on the size you use.

Lay the chicken halves on the mesh grid over the fire and barbecue. Baste with a sauce and turn them about every five minutes, using basting brushes and picnic forks with very long handles. Allow about 45 minutes for the smaller size chickens and an hour for larger ones.

A basting sauce for the chicken is made of 1 quart of water, 2 quarts of vinegar, 2 pounds of butter, ½ cup salt, 1 tablespoon each pepper and paprika. Keep this mixture hot and stir it frequently as you use it.

CLAM BAKE

A clam bake doesn't have to be given on a sandy, rocky beach but it helps in preparing the pit. For a crowd of 50 people you'll need a pit about 2½x2½ feet square and a foot deep. In addition, you'll need to collect plenty of rounded dry stones the size of a small head of cabbage or lettuce.

Line the pit with a layer of the stones, then cover them with fire wood, any of the hardwoods recommended on page 153 for pit barbecuing. Light the fire, then add alternate layers of stones and wood until the pile is about 3 feet high and allow it to burn 2 or 3 hours or until the whole heap has settled into the ash pit and the stones are very hot.

Now rake away the embers and cover the rocks with a six-inch layer of seaweed. Next, spread the clams over the seaweed. You'll need about 3 bushels for 50 people. Follow this with another layer of seaweed, one lobster for each guest, then sweet corn, potatoes and onions, enough for everyone, with a final layer of seaweed. Finally over the top, put a wet canvas or tarpaulin.

Fasten it down securely around the edges with more stones to prevent steam escaping.

Now let 'er cook an hour or longer. To test whether the food is done, pull out a lobster near the edge of the pile. When it is cooked all the food is ready. Remove the canvas and seaweed and let the guests dig in. Be sure to have plenty of melted butter for the clams, lobsters and corn.

LUAU

This party, patterned after the famous Hawaiian luaus, is perhaps the most glamorous of all outdoor parties. To be truly authentic, a tablecloth is laid on the ground and completely covered with large fern leaves. Food is eaten with fingers; no plates, knives or forks are used. The traditional main dish, a whole young pig filled with hot rocks is cooked in an imu, a pit similar to a deep pit, but with banana leaves covering the coals. Accompanying dishes are bananas and sweet potatoes wrapped and cooked in ti leaves.

Banana and ti leaves may be difficult to come by but, this need not deter you from having a luau feast. Serve your luau American-style. Your guests may be happier eating foods from plates with knives and forks and they may prefer to sit at tables rather than on the ground. But, no matter how food is eaten or where guests sit, be sure to cover tablecloth with fern leaves.

If you have an abundance of small flowers, your guests will get the spirit of the party if each, on arrival, receives a lei. Make them by stringing flowers together on a strong thread using a heavy needle. Pinks, carnations, asters, daisies, pompoms, dahlias, chrysanthemums and red and white clover are a few of the flowers which are easiest to string. Serve fruit punch and, plenty of it before and during the meal. When spiked with rum it's truly Hawaiian!

Barbecue the pig in an open pit as directed on page

153 or barbecue it on a spit according to directions on page 64. Serve it with sweet potatoes and bananas, wrapped and cooked in foil. See pages 110 and 114 for preparing them.

For an even simpler adaptation of the luau, prepare the foods on a battery of portable braziers. If your own supply of units is limited, perhaps some of your guests will bring theirs along. They'll be glad to when they hear what's in store!

Many recipes in this book are particularly well suited to this kind of party. Some of them are, Grilled Spareribs (page 28) with Sweet-Sour Basting Sauce (page 126), Barbecued Chicken Halves with Easy Basting Sauce (page 37), Sesame Sea Food (page 90) and Bar-B-Qued Bananas (page 114). You might want to add fruit kebobs either as an accompaniment or a dessert. Three such recipes are on page 93. Other dessert ideas are Lemon Coconut (page 144), Orange Sherbet or ice cream and coffee.

INDEX